'In the digital age, when spellchecking is almost universal, it is easy to forget the essential role of learning to spell in becoming literate. In this update to her book, Lyn Stone reminds us that learning to spell is more than just the tedious task of memorizing lists of words. Learning to spell is the partner of learning to read, each enhancing and dependent on the other. Lyn not only reminds us of the importance of spelling, but shows us how to teach it in a way that fits with learning to read and matches what we know about how young brains become literate.'

Steven P. Dykstra, PhD, Psychologist and Member of the International Foundation for Effective Reading Instruction & CORELearn National Advisory Board

'We used to teach spelling more effectively, but since whole language, balanced literacy and multi-cueing reading instruction has dominated classrooms, teaching spelling has been replaced by approaches that rely on visual memory; a very inefficient strategy. You cannot teach what you do not know, so as an academic who works with pre-service and experienced teachers, who can rarely explain why words are spelled the way they are, *Spelling for Life* will provide the lesson plan, words and knowledge to make explicit how to teach the conventions of the writing system.'

Dr Lorraine Hammond, PhD CF AM, Associate Professor, Edith Cowan University, Australia

'Lyn Stone has done the (almost) impossible! With technical accuracy and scientific precision, she provides an approach that makes spelling your friend. When you look for a friend, don't you want someone reliable and predictable, as well as fun and interesting? Lyn's masterful description of the English writing system shows spelling in that light. Learning how to spell well becomes fascinating and approachable. And Lyn offers instructors a framework that weaves spelling into a larger literacy context. Not only will students have improved spelling, but their ability to read and express themselves is bound to grow too, with careful attention paid to the many layers of our complex language.'

Sara Peden, R. Psych, Member Ontario College of Teachers

SPELLING FOR LIFE

There is a myth that English spelling is unnecessarily complex, and it is spread by those who don't understand the writing system. *Spelling for Life* offers lucid, accessible tools which help to reveal that, when explicitly and systematically taught, spelling is scientific, law-abiding and even elegant.

Using a synthesis of theory, research and teaching experience, the fascinating nature of English spelling is systematically teased out. The examples and exercises throughout offer an encouraging, accessible way to implement the program of study and strive to reveal the beauty of spelling. *Spelling for Life* enables teachers and students to

- learn what the common spelling coping strategies are;
- gain insights into undoing poor spelling habits;
- work together to reveal patterns not only in regular spelling, but also in words which on the surface seem to break the spelling rules;
- practise successful spelling strategies, progressing from simple to complex words rapidly and with confidence.

This new and improved edition includes updated spelling techniques as well as new chapters on *orthographic mapping, spelling assessment, teaching consonant clusters well* and *suffixing rules.* Aided by example lessons, formative assessments, unique tools, a scope and sequence, and extensive practice lists, this highly acclaimed overview of spelling succeeds in developing theory and practice in the writing system for teacher and student alike.

Lyn Stone is a linguist and author in private practice. She lives and works in Victoria, Australia, where she runs her education consultancy, Lifelong Literacy. Her goal is to help teachers awaken linguistic curiosity in their students using creative, engaging tools and strategies, based upon scientific consensus as to what constitutes best practice.

SPELLING FOR LIFE

Uncovering the Simplicity and Science of Spelling

Second edition

Lyn Stone

Routledge
Taylor & Francis Group

LONDON AND NEW YORK

Second edition published 2021
by Routledge
2 Park Square, Milton Park, Abingdon, Oxon OX14 4RN

and by Routledge
52 Vanderbilt Avenue, New York, NY 10017

Routledge is an imprint of the Taylor & Francis Group, an informa business

© 2021 Lyn Stone

First edition published by Routledge 2014

British Library Cataloguing-in-Publication Data
A catalogue record for this book is available from the British Library

Library of Congress Cataloging-in-Publication Data
Names: Stone, Lyn, 1971- author.
Title: Spelling for life: uncovering the simplicity and science of spelling/Lyn Stone.
Description: Abingdon, Oxon; New York, NY: Routledge, 2021. |
Includes bibliographical references and index. |
Identifiers: LCCN 2020044230 |
ISBN 9780367646561 (hardback) | ISBN 9780367645694 (paperback) |
ISBN 9781003125686 (ebook)
Subjects: LCSH: English language–Orthography and spelling–Study and teaching (Primary)
Classification: LCC LB1526.S76 2021 | DDC 372.63/2-dc23
LC record available at https://lccn.loc.gov/2020044230

ISBN: 978-0-367-64656-1 (hbk)
ISBN: 978-0-367-64569-4 (pbk)
ISBN: 978-1-003-12568-6 (ebk)

Typeset in Interstate
by Deanta Global Publishing Services, Chennai, India

For my family

CONTENTS

LIST OF TABLES & FIGURES

FOREWORD

I could never have imagined that I would one day agree to recommend a book espousing principles so contrary to my own as *Spelling for Life*. I believe that English spelling is inconsistent, too burdened with its medieval heritage, and therefore sometimes unmanageable, while Lyn Stone assures us that it is 'an elegant, pattern-based system, which becomes apparent if examined thoughtfully.' But then I engage in quixotic battles for spelling reform, a reform that will, I am afraid, never be carried out (implemented, as her Scottish kin might say), while she has devoted years to teaching children, dyslexic children among them, how to spell and has achieved laudable results. I have nothing but admiration for her efforts, even though my views on English spelling remain unaltered. But perhaps there is greater honor (allow me to stick to American spelling and grammar in this Foreword) in receiving praise from an opponent than from a member of one's own party.

At a time when the sons of English gentlemen were routinely sent to public (that is, private) schools, so at least until the 1890s, some of their textbooks bore titles like *Exercises in Etymology* and *Lessons in Etymology*. Those manuals had very little to do with etymology as we today understand it, because their subject matter was grammar (morphology with elements of syntax) and word formation. *Spelling for Life* reminds me of those useful books. Today few people remember them, but at an age in which English grammar was supposed to replicate the grammar of Latin, they must have served their purpose well. The young Winston Churchill was still made to 'decline' the noun *table* so: nominative (*table*), genitive (*of the table*), dative (*to the table*), accusative (*table*), ablative (*by the table*), and vocative (*o table*). He was puzzled by the vocative, but that form, the examiner told him, occurred when he apostrophised a table, which, by his admittance, he never did.

In the early twentieth century, thanks to the efforts of many prominent linguists, children (no longer only boys!) began to study English grammar along modern lines. All went reasonably well until somebody – not too long ago – discovered that grammar was boring and not 'fun.' Fun, the backbone of modern instruction in all areas, banished grammar. So today's undergraduates swoon when they hear the phrase *subjunctive mood outside subordinate clauses*. But experience shows that, when teachers know how to do things properly, the audience, regardless of the level, understands and enjoys grammar and 'etymology' in all its aspects.

Spelling for Life is informed with the spirit of optimism and the author's belief in children's ability and readiness to master difficulties. Every page in it is based on experience and convinces the user that, indeed, a language system can and should be presented to a class of eager learners and that the presentation will bear fruit. Step by step, Lyn Stone goes through vowels, consonants, and syllable structure; introduces such concepts as homophones; touches on the role of foreign elements in English (this would be etymology by any definition); explains the meaning of exceptions, which often also follow rules; and reveals laws where, at first sight, lawlessness reigns supreme.

Perhaps no evidence is needed to prove that English spelling can be mastered. After all, most of us end up as tolerably good spellers (in this respect, English-speakers do not differ from their French, German, or Russian counterparts), though I know no one who would not sometimes be in doubt about the shape of words like *reconstructable* (isn't it *reconstructible*?), *schism*, *skeptic*, *ascetic*, or *chthonic*. Those, however, are negligible crumbs. The real pie is more digestible. Even if we agree that English spelling is an elegant, pattern-based system of writing, the pattern requires an earnest effort to learn, and we would perhaps be better off if *quarter* were spelled *kwarter*, *unscathed* were spelled *unskathed*, and *gnaw* lost its initial *g*. (And what about *Lin* for *Lyn*?) But let me repeat: This is not an issue for Lyn Stone. She has an artifact before her, enjoys its complex beauty, and wants to open her pupils' eyes to it. In this she has succeeded in an exemplary way; her book is practical from first page to last. Her enthusiasm is contagious, and the uses to which her work can be put will be obvious to every unprejudiced teacher.

In principle, *Spelling for Life* can be consulted anywhere in the English-speaking world, given an enthusiastic instructor and a malleable class. But whom have bad instructors taught anything, and what have those learned who fought their teachers? Teaching is like love: it brings happiness only if it is requited. I wish the book loving users and a long life on library shelves and especially in the classroom.

Anatoly Liberman,
author of the weekly column 'The Oxford Etymologist'

PREFACE

Sexy jobs for linguists

I'm sure you've seen television crime shows where some clever linguist analyses a voice pattern or a sample of handwriting and helps the detectives catch the criminal.

Forensic linguistics is what I call one of the 'sexy' careers for linguists. I'm not even sure it exists.

Another sexy career is being an accent consultant for Hollywood movies. The existence of this job is also somewhat doubtful if the dialogue in *Braveheart* is anything to go by.

Fantasy jobs aside, some linguists don't even get to use their degrees directly in their careers, such is the nature of employment in our modern world.

I am very lucky, then, to have been able to use my degree in my career from the moment I graduated until the present day. This has been the source of some of my life's greatest pleasures.

Not long after obtaining my B.A. and moving to Australia, I was lucky enough to land a job in a Lindamood-Bell clinic in Sydney. Their training in the Lindamood Phoneme Sequencing (LiPS) Program was an unbelievably dense, exceptionally vivid example of how to use linguistics to change literacy and, as a consequence, lives.

A few years later, my Spalding training at the Speech, Language and Literacy Centre, under the peerless tutelage of Mary-Ruth Reed, deepened and broadened my knowledge of linguistics as it applies to literacy in countless ways.

Over those years, it came to my notice that those who struggled with spelling, and not necessarily other components of literacy, had sets of pattern-based habits predictable from a relatively small example of their writing.

Coupled with this, there were times when it was impossible to deliver the very complex and time-consuming Lindamood and/or Spalding programs to their full extent. I kept having to ask myself, 'Which principles are going to give this learner the biggest bang for their buck?'

The answer always seemed to follow the same general pattern. I began to collate my clinical notes and noticed that the path to spelling improvement always took certain turns.

This path evolved into handouts and informal knowledge-sharing with my colleagues until it began to emerge as a consistent, cohesive set of lesson plans and charts.

Deciding to take this knowledge further, I began consulting to schools and holding seminars and developed a work-in-progress called 'Spelling for Life'.

I don't claim to be an academic linguist by any means, having obtained my B.A. in 1994, but I do feel that I have been allowed to continuously put into practice all the wonderful theory taught to me about the structure of language. It is my privilege to be able to observe how language works on a daily basis and to have the chance to help figure out what to do when a particular aspect isn't working.

This is my attempt to help figure out what to do when spelling isn't working, or at least to help prevent spelling from not working.

This edition has some updated terminology, new chapters informed by the science of learning, notes on assessment, and a suggested scope and sequence to help with schoolwide implementation.

ACKNOWLEDGEMENTS

Without the sacrifices my mother and father made to bring me up all over the world and put me through a first-class school education, I might never have become interested in linguistics.

Without the top-quality tuition and brilliance of Dick Hudson and the Linguistics department at UCL, I might never have gained the knowledge necessary to write this book.

Without the deep and broad expertise of geniuses in their fields, Phyllis Lindamood and Mary-Ruth Mendel, I might never have figured out how to put all this knowledge together to write this book.

Without the courage, humour, and dedication of my wonderful students, who laughed at my silly jokes and let me do experiments on them, I might never have been able to shape this book into something useful.

Without the kind support and great advice of my publisher, Bruce Roberts, I doubt I would have had so many golden opportunities to write about what I love and to keep updating that.

Without the patience, encouragement, and unconditional love of my husband Byron, I might never have had the time and space to use that knowledge to write this book. He's really good at I.T. as well, which has helped enormously.

My beautiful girls have not only provided me with a first-hand perspective on child language acquisition, but have continued to be awfully well-behaved while I developed this and other books.

Without the patient, gentle, but direct and ever-so-rapid critiques from my teachers and fellows Chris Burdess, Fiona Duffy, and Rex Harley, I might never have had the confidence to let this book be what it is.

Many thanks also to my pedantic proofers and processors, Tony Greenwood, Gez Runham, Kenny Reay, David Squire, and David McKenzie.

And finally, for the unflinching feedback, consistent support, and highly instructive, enlightening, and entertaining dialogue on the nature of pedagogy, I would also like to thank the Australian schools and teachers who have provided me with the impetus over all these years to keep writing this book.

SOUND TO SYMBOL NOTATION

Rather than use the International Phonetic Alphabet (IPA), which is adorable, but would force the reader to learn a whole new set of symbols, the major vowel sounds in this book are represented by the following notation:

/a/ as in 'cat'
/ay/ as in 'day'
/ah/ as in 'bath' (in some accents but not mine)
/e/ as in 'get'
/ee/ as in 'see'
/i/ as in 'sit'
/ie/ as in die
/o/ as in 'not'
/oe/ as in 'toe'
/u/ as in 'gum'
/ue/ as in 'cue'
/oo/ as in 'too'
/uu/ as in 'put'
/oy/ as in 'boy'
/ou/ as in 'house'

The vowel sounds above are based on a standard English accent. We have to start somewhere, and we might as well start with a common, relatable English accent.

The only IPA symbols used are /ə/ (Chapter 23) and /ʒ/ (Chapter 26). For reasons that will become clear, they are necessary and unavoidable.

Types of bracketing

<> angle brackets are used to surround alphabet letters. When the reader sees them, it is a signal for them to say the letters within, e.g. the letter <s> is also a suffix.

'' single quotation marks are used to surround example words.

// slanted brackets are used to surround sounds. When the reader sees them, it is a signal for them to say the sound those letters represent, e.g. the letter <c> makes a /s/ sound before <e>.

- the dash is to represent an incomplete word. It indicates that there is at least one letter or one syllable in its place, e.g. let's write some more -ble words or the prefix re- means 'back' or 'again'.

INTRODUCTION

Whilst I acknowledge that it is possible to find spelling difficult and that it can appear complex, I cannot agree that it is unpredictable or random.

I find the field of automotive mechanics difficult and complex, but I know it takes no more than average intelligence and a lot of learning and practice to master it. Nobody calls that random.

Some people are natural mechanics and, with some practice, can take to it with ease. Others have less aptitude and need to start at the very beginning and work their way through the subject.

I actually don't know any field of knowledge that isn't like this, yet spelling has such a bad reputation.

I would like to offer a means of taking this much-maligned and misunderstood subject and viewing it as a scientific system that evolved through various processes of selection to become an elegant, stable, law-abiding and satisfying means of communication. You just have to know certain things about it, and it is best to learn those things in a certain order.

By calling spelling beautiful and elegant, perhaps I'm imposing my own aesthetic sense onto it, but I think a balance is due.

Those who are natural spellers don't spell well by accident. They have learned certain things. This book is an attempt to focus on those things.

It is not a panacea that will cure all learning difficulties, but at the very least, the lessons strive to impart core (not basic) knowledge.

Basic knowledge (phonics) is taught, in most modern school systems, in the first two years.

This book is about teaching core knowledge in the years subsequent to that and can be used from that point onwards and even in secondary and adult learning settings.

Teaching spelling is not so much to do with being able to explain all the rules and have all the reasons for exceptions readily available, but it's about making the decision to construct spelling lessons that help students 'look under the bonnet' of our writing system.

Much emphasis is placed on discovering why some words are exceptional, and in that discovery, we help to reveal a deeper rule-structure and thus avoid having to revert to the 'just because ...' explanation of irregular words.

> Spelling is a scientific system that evolved through various processes of selection to become an elegant, stable, law-abiding, and satisfying means of communication. You just have to know certain things about, it and it is best to learn those things in a certain order.

What things and in what order?

There are 30 chapters in this book, mostly comprising self-contained lessons.

Some can be taught at any stage, as they do not require anything but the ability to listen and respond, some require a grounding in phonics and handwriting skills, and some require all this as well as word and world knowledge commensurate with mainstream middle primary children. Each chapter has a lesson plan specifying the skill level required.

The penultimate chapter is a suggested scope and sequence beginning in the foundation year.

Links to supporting videos

Many chapters and lessons are supported by free videos that show examples of teaching the concepts in the book. You do not have to view these videos to be able to teach the lessons. Links to these constantly updated videos can be found on the Lifelong Literacy website (www.lifelongliteracy.com).

Patterns to discover

One of the unique qualities of *Spelling for Life* is that it was created knowing that English spelling follows stable, predictable patterns, just like mathematics. Each concept reveals a pattern.

Discovering these patterns can be a profoundly enriching experience for students. The patterns to be discovered are listed in the lesson plans.

Lesson plans

Each lesson has a step-by-step plan which includes notes on prerequisite knowledge, materials, and approximate duration.

Most of the lessons have worksheet resources that can be printed, enlarged if necessary, and distributed. Examples of completed worksheets are also included where necessary.

Wherever appropriate, the lesson plans mention the typical error pattern that the lesson is attempting to erase. Spelling errors are often pattern-based and are the result of habits or coping strategies that *can* be undone.

Example lessons

When I was being trained to deliver various literacy programs, time and time again I wished that I could instantly say the exact words that my teachers said to their students. They made teaching these programs look so easy.

This is why I have provided example lessons. These lessons are in a conversational style typical of one that I would have with my students. Familiarise yourself with these if you wish, and by all means feel free to adapt them to your own style. They are merely there to help.

In the example lessons, answers to all questions are capitalised in brackets after the question.

The questions and answers will look like this:

How many letters are in the alphabet? (26)
How many of those are vowels? (5)
What are they? (A, E, I, O, U)
So all the rest are consonants.

Ownwork

The general pattern in *Spelling for Life* is to set a piece of 'ownwork' for every rule or concept delivered. This usually consists of finding examples of and exceptions to rules.

The ownwork is restricted to single-word exercises, as these are the building blocks of all the other language-arts activities your students will experience in their daily lives.

If students genuinely have trouble finding words for the tasks, it is okay to help them by suggesting words they could use.

Spelling drills

At the end of many chapters there is a spelling drill, designed to be used as a brief check for understanding. These are dictated orally and scored.

The drills show students their progress. They also give you an idea of what, if anything, you might need to revise and help you with your lesson planning.

Differentiation

You can distribute blank or partially filled worksheets, depending on the skill level of your students.

Lists and examples

None of the lists included here are exhaustive or exclusive of any other list. They have simply been compiled over many years in the practice as my personal store of examples.

Spelling lessons often require example words from students. It is my strong suggestion that whenever possible, the definition of the example word is also provided, e.g., if a student suggests a word that doesn't fall into the first few hundred vocabulary words on most wordlists, by all means accept it, but also ask for a definition. If the definition isn't known, take the time to look it up in a good dictionary, noting etymology if possible.

This simple tactic not only demonstrates excellent vocabulary-building habits, but enriches and strengthens your students' vocabularies exponentially. Take each word as an opportunity for exploration and you will be the teacher responsible for opening your students' eyes to the depth and breadth of our language.

1 Orthographic mapping

How do children become fluent readers and writers? They do so by building up a store of words they can recognise effortlessly, without sounding them out and without looking elsewhere for cues. In fact, once they have a word in their sight word vocabulary, they cannot suppress its sound and possible meanings when they come to that word again.

This is the most useful meaning of the phrase *sight word*. There are some who define sight words as 'words that do not follow simple phoneme–grapheme correspondence rules'. Words like 'eye' and 'could', 'would', 'should', etc. might fall into this category. However, this type of word is better described as *irregular*.

Irregular words are only classified as irregular until their structure has been analyzed and explained. All words are spelled the way they are for a reason. Unfamiliar spellings only *seem* irregular.

Another common but inaccurate definition of sight words is 'words which need to be learned by looking at the whole word and memorizing it as a whole'. This look-say method of teaching reading grew like a noxious weed in education in the last century. It was based on the erroneous assumption that storage and retrieval of words is an act of visual memory. It is not. Our eyes are the first processors when encountering words, that is true, but research has shown that word storage and retrieval are not functions of the visual system (Kilpatrick 2016). A blind person would not be able to learn to read if vision were the key driver in word learning.

In actual fact, it is the hearing-impaired population that gets the raw deal when learning to read, since so much of the early foundations for literacy are laid using the auditory, not visual, system.

Irregular or not, how *are* words memorised in the first place? Think about the massive amount of words and word parts you recognise instantly. Did you consciously memorise every single word you ever encountered? Let's place it into perspective: The average literate adult can automatically recognise between 30,000 and 70,000 words and word parts (Kilpatrick 2016). Did we do some kind of memorisation trick 70,000 times? Did someone teach us every single one? No, that would be impossible.

What we did was use orthographic mapping and self-teaching to gain our permanent sight word vocabulary.

Linnea Ehri, a researcher at the University of California, spent much of her time focusing on this process and coined the term *orthographic mapping* (Ehri 2014).

When learning to read, children need to be taught to look at the sequence of letters on the page, translate them into possible phonemes that they represent, and then blend those phonemes to form pronunciations of whole words.

So they map the symbols, to the sounds, to the words. The letter represents the sound, which, in conjunction with the other letters and sounds, represents the word. These sequences then become bonded, eventually resulting in effortless decoding, regardless of how complex the pattern is. So a word like *straight* can be stored just as efficiently as *cat*, if the person has highly developed orthographic mapping skills (Figure 1.1).

Ehri's key findings

- Children who have good knowledge of grapheme–phoneme correspondences can retain words in their long-term memory with more efficiency than those who don't.
- Underpinning this proficiency is phonemic awareness.
- The crucial part of this kind of memorisation is attention to the *sequence* of letters in a word.
- This builds cumulatively and eventually results in seemingly effortless decoding of familiar and, more importantly, unfamiliar or irregular words.

This is where Share's Self-Teaching Hypothesis comes in.

Share's Self-Teaching Hypothesis

There comes a point in a student's life that I call *the sweet spot*. It's where, after sometimes many hours, weeks, or months of seemingly endless effort, they begin to read unfamiliar words without them being explicitly taught.

According to psychologist and researcher David L. Share, students with sufficient phonological awareness and phonics knowledge begin to apply those skills to novel words and start to independently bond those sequences into long-term memory. This is known as *phonological recoding* (Share 1995).

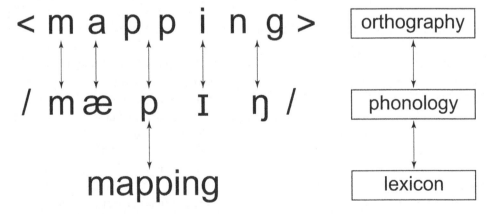

Figure 1.1 Orthographic mapping diagram

The important point is that again, the process involves *phonological* recoding. It cannot take place without attention to phonology, conscious or not.

It stands to reason, then, that acquisition of novel words, and eventually of literacy overall, relies on taking that phonological route. Guessing, skipping, looking at pictures, or memorising whole words on flashcards interferes with this process. It is especially disastrous for spelling.

Some ideas for teaching to enhance orthographic mapping

Think carefully about your grouping technique

Group words to be learned as a spelling focus into close, logical families.

This can be done along orthographic, etymological, or morphological lines (and those lines often overlap). Be careful though, when attempting to group words along phonological lines. Grouping them by *sound* alone is inefficient, given that there can be multiple spellings for one sound.

Words are spelled the way they are because of where they came from and which families they belong to. Grouping by sound essentially ignores all of that rich, generalizable information.

In terms of cognitive load, lists containing multiple spellings place far too much pressure on working memory. A successful system for learning spelling is one which pays attention to cognitive load and pace.

Figure 1.2 is an example of a word list, grouped by sound, that violates the principles of cognitive load, explicit instruction, and a systematic approach.

Trying to teach spelling this way is like trying to teach biology by saying, 'Let's memorise all the things with legs'.

The unfortunate child who was given the list in Figure 1.2, to cram for a Friday test, was asked to memorise words in the first section. The children in his class who weren't particularly struggling with spelling were asked to memorise the middle words. The words in the last section were for the good spellers only. No definitions, no structure, no morphology, nothing

	POOR SPELLERS	MIDDLE SPELLERS	GOOD SPELLERS
d dd as in **duck**	adopt, needle, deathly, remained, advice, addition, developer, declare, period	destructive, rendezvous, dissension, discernible, appendicitis, additive, endeavour, superintendent, dependent, dependant,	candidate, decisive, democracy, determination, dawdle, durable, condemnation, deteriorate, descendant, rendezvous

Figure 1.2 An example of very low-quality spelling instruction

was offered in the way of study of these words. And the teacher would happily say she was 'doing phonics', not because she was a bad *teacher*, but because her teaching degree placed no importance on the structure of language and failed to come into the 21st century in terms of reading science.

Close families, related by more than just their sounds, will win every time.

Don't discount copying

Develop your students' ability to copy efficiently. Copying words, sentences, and paragraphs is not only a great way to practise fluency and spelling, using a scaffolded, stable framework, but also, if used purposefully, can enhance everything else that constitutes writing.

Establish productive practice routines

Drill new words, first by sounding each phoneme whilst following the sequence of the letters, and then by saying the whole word.

Please don't ask students to write the words over and over again. Anyone who has ever had the punishment of writing lines knows that after a few repetitions, those words become scratches on a page and lose all their meaning.

There is also the distinct possibility of error reinforcement if the original word was transcribed wrongly.

To map words efficiently, students have to attend to their pronunciation in combination with the sequence of letters in the word.

Interleaving the target words throughout your teaching sequence also leads to efficient mapping. Use the words in copied/dictated sentences and paragraphs.

Have students compose sentences and paragraphs containing the words. Review all the words regularly. Break the habit of issuing the words on Monday and testing on Friday, never to be looked at again.

Meaning is key

Define and use each word in a sentence when teaching them. If you don't provide definitions, the words might as well be in Swahili or Dothraki. How will students develop their awareness of the writing system otherwise? Words are related to one another, and those relationships are driven by meaning. Divorce words from their definitions and you also sever the path to the full richness of the writing system.

How low-quality literacy instruction leads to poor spelling

Due to the fact that letters in words appear in sequences, any instructional method that takes attention away from the sequences will interfere with efficient orthographic mapping. Some widely used examples are the following:

- Students are sometimes encouraged to guess words by looking away from unfamiliar words, especially if they are prompted to look at pictures instead of the word. Looking at the letters in the words in the correct sequence is not only the habit of good readers, but is also the process that creates good spellers.

- Students are often encouraged to develop the habit of skipping unfamiliar words: No analysis leads to no memory.
- Students are often encouraged to only look at the first letter of a word: Partial analysis leads to partial recall.
- There are some teaching frameworks that make a big deal of asking students not to point to words as they read. This is horrible. As a literate adult, I still point to words on the page if I want to read them very carefully (think legal documents and complex instructions). Taking that support away from children is ludicrous and based on zero research.
- In the initial stages, providing reading material that doesn't match the sequence of grapheme-phoneme correspondences being introduced also impairs orthographic mapping. How do children get exposure to what you've taught if the practice material contains unfamiliar patterns?
- The way a word looks is the least memorable feature of a word. Getting students to do exercises based on visual features of words is a waste of practice time. The letter sequences, bonded to their pronunciations, not their colour, shape, or spacing in between, is what the mind stores and recognises.

2 Spelling assessment

Assessment is the key to placement and progress monitoring in the cooperative journey towards better spelling that you and your students share.

If you are going to make an effort to teach something, then it stands to reason that you need to check that your students understand and can apply what you have taught. If they can, they have been taught well. If they can't, valid and reliable assessment helps you to quickly find out why they can't and either re-teach or recommend further testing.

At our practice, we use a variety of spelling placement and progress monitoring tests. The complexity of skills and processes involved in the act of writing is awe-inspiring. Making time to check each skill separately *and* combined is the hallmark of an effective system.

We also assess phonological awareness, listening comprehension, single-word reading, and letter-sound reading and writing. We do this to gain an overall insight into the student's profile.

We use these assessments at different times, and we interleave the words we are studying through review and homework assignments. Overall, we are careful about monitoring progress, and we are realistic about what can and can't be achieved. Sometimes we work with children whose spelling ability is so severely impaired, as in cases of dyslexia and dysgraphia and/or very low quality early reading instruction, that we have to advocate for accommodations and manage teacher and parent expectations.

What we never do is imply that a child's spelling is 'atrocious', or that if they had more 'confidence' or 'worked a bit harder' or were less 'careless', they would be better spellers. Children don't misspell words on purpose.

Neither do we promote the myth that English spelling is idiosyncratic or opaque. We measure, teach, and measure again. Progress is a direct result of our teaching skill within the parameters of the students' cognitive profile. Valid and reliable assessment is the key to it all.

Our main single-word test is the *Morrison McCall Spelling Scale*. We use this test because of its high validity and reliability. It consists of eight separate 50-item single-word tests. This means that you can run the test eight times before repeating a word.

The stopping rule is five consecutive errors, but there's also a starting rule once the initial test has been done. Say the students spelled the first ten items correctly in a previous test, the next test would start at item number eight instead of number one. This guards against fatigue and measures what is supposed to be measured, i.e. single-word spelling, not stamina, attention, or self-regulation.

The test also relates to a 2,300-item word list called the *Ayres Word List* from the *Spalding Writing Road to Reading* program (a highly recommended treasure trove of excellent instruction). Though I'm not a fan of word lists per se, this is a good guide to the type of material at that should be covered at each stage. The *Morrison McCall Spelling Scale* will tell teachers where to start within that list.

The test also gives an approximate grade level, and because of the eight-test battery, progress can be reliably monitored over time.

Finally, the test, like any single-word spelling test, also gives us information about how well a child transcribes. Error and handwriting analysis informs much of what we teach and helps us make decisions about further referral if necessary.

We also monitor spelling choice by giving tests that ask students to choose between two words, one misspelled and the other correctly spelled, such as 'kwest' vs. 'quest'. This is a good predictor of reading ability (Marinus et al. 2012), but for our clinical population, it also helps us to predict a student's response to spelling intervention.

An orthographic choice test offers great insight into spelling potential. For instance, say two students had the same low score on a single-word spelling test. Would that mean that they would respond to intervention in the same way? Not necessarily. A spelling choice test would give a finer-grained profile. The student who scores higher in a choice test will likely respond to spelling intervention better than the student who scores poorly. This is because a higher score indicates a clearer concept of what 'looks right' in English words.

In fact, when students score very poorly on this sort of test, we make it a priority to advocate for this student at school and with their carers. A low score indicates that their ability to edit their work will be much lower than an average student. It is not carelessness or lack of confidence or, heaven help us, *laziness* that is causing this student to hand in error-laden written work. It goes much deeper than that and should be recognised, cared about, and acknowledged. Spell-checking software is a reasonable, if not crucial, accommodation for a student with this particular profile.

On the other hand, higher scores on a word choice test can show that students can indeed spot errors adequately in their written work and should be asked to take care when editing. Even if they can't yet produce the correct spelling, they at least have a fair chance of knowing what to look up.

As a method of formative assessment, students are given short dictation passages during our sessions. We use a mix of ready made passages, which roughly correspond to a range of grade levels, alongside passages composed on the spot to directly target words that have been taught in previous lessons.

Because dictation involves transcription but not text generation, it is slightly harder than a single-word spelling test but easier than a composition. From this we gain insight into words and orthographic patterns that students have not achieved automaticity with. This then forms the plan for subsequent lessons.

3 Broken rules and word stories

There is a common myth that English spelling is hard to learn. Many of our words don't have a 1:1 sound to symbol match, that is true, but the vast majority do conform to predictable rules. Chomsky and Halle (1968) and C. Chomsky (1970) refer to English spelling as 'optimal', in terms of conveying both sound and meaning. That's a good sign. The problem is that it is tempting to be frightened of words which aren't predictable by the better-known rules.

Cognitive psychologist and linguist Steven Pinker describes our writing system thus:

> But though writing is an artificial contraption connecting vision and language, it must tap into the language system at well-demarcated points, and that gives it a modicum of logic.
>
> (Pinker 1994)

Exceptions

The lessons in this book are constructed not only to illustrate the core rules of English spelling but also to encourage discussion of exceptions. The idea is to get students to revel in the exceptions. Too often, a student is proud to learn and demonstrate a rule, only to be confounded by an exception. Looking for exceptions leads to confidence in the rules and ideally to the realisation that English spelling and reading is easier than initially thought.

In many cases, words which don't 'play fair' (i.e. that appear to break the core rules) are common, so a student is likely to run into an exception very quickly. The only way round this is to boldly announce that there are exceptions to every rule and that they should be celebrated. This will not only build confidence and reinforce these very important rules, but will also build vocabulary and strengthen the ability to investigate.

Words which break the core rules do so for certain basic reasons that not only reflect past influences (their word story), but also highlight the ever-changing nature of language.

> There is a common myth that English spelling is hard to learn. Many of our words don't have a 1:1 sound-to-symbol match, that is true, but the vast majority do conform to predictable rules.

We will, then, examine regular and seemingly irregular words and do several things with them:

- Notice which rule applies or is broken;
- Investigate the reason for the perceived break, i.e. the word story;
- Assign the words to groups that share common characteristics, what we will call *word families.*

Before pattern and core rule study begins, it is important to understand why certain words appear to break the rules and how to tackle them.

The seven major stories of exceptional words are:

1 Borrowed words – as we move toward globalisation, words from other languages continue to swell our lexicon ('spaghetti', 'ski', 'haiku').
2 Abbreviations – words which, when shortened, break conventional spelling rules ('rev' from 'revolution', 'taxi' from 'taxicab', 'mini' from 'miniature').
3 Acronyms – words made from the first letter or letters of other words ('Qantas', 'lol', etc.).
4 Names – place names often break the core rules because they belong to other languages with other sets of rules ('Iraq', 'Benghazi'). Human names often don't conform because they are created through a process of parental invention rather than linguistic evolution ('Dannii', 'Keanu').
5 Jargon – technical/scientific vocabulary ('radii', 'caesarean', 'schwa').
6 Old and/or common – words that are obeying rules from times past, whose spelling hasn't caught up with the way we say them ('of', 'colonel', 'one').
7 Slang – vocabulary used by a particular generation of younger speakers or groups ('chav', 'wassup', 'ermahgerd').

Or BAANJOS, as I like to remember them (said in a Southern US accent to help me remember the extra <a>).

Lesson plan

Skill level

This lesson can be done as soon as students start reading and writing words.

Materials

- Figure 3.1 Word stories example worksheet
- Figure 3.2 Word stories blank worksheet

Pattern

When words appear to break the rules, it is because they entered our language by one of seven major paths. These paths are the word's 'story'.

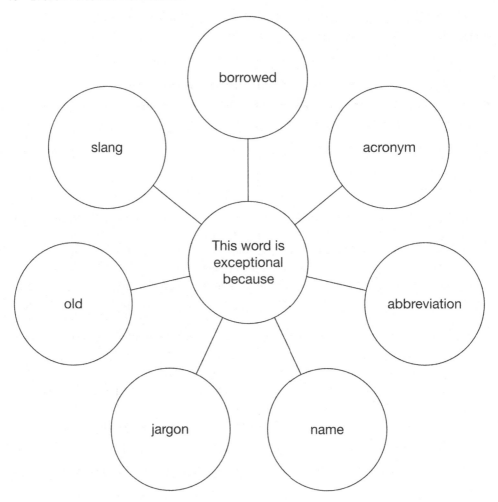

Figure 3.1 Word stories example worksheet

Error pattern

Defeatism, or the belief that spelling is random.

Duration

10 minutes per word story. Not all stories have to be done at once.

Step 1

You can either have a target word in mind when you deliver this lesson, or you can just use the lesson to introduce the idea that there are exceptions to rules in spelling.

Distribute a word stories blank worksheet (Figure 3.2). Explain that examining how a word entered our language (its story) helps us understand why some words don't 'play fair'.

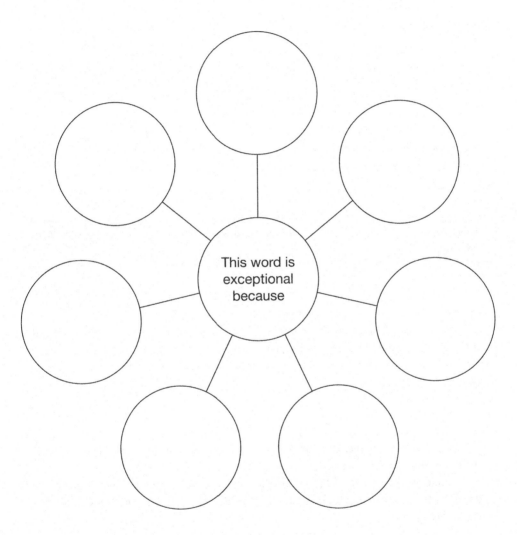

Figure 3.2 Word stories blank worksheet

Step 2

Brainstorm the word stories and write them in the worksheet with examples. You might only come up with a couple of stories at this point. Refer back to this sheet as they occur. You can print multiple sheets for all the different lessons and you may also want to create a large, central word stories worksheet for display in the classroom.

Example lesson

To help us understand why some words look like they don't play fair, let's look at their stories.

Brainstorm any stories your students already know and write examples. When it comes to number six, the 'old' category, a little more discussion is required.

There are two main ways in which we use language. What are they? (SPEAKING AND WRITING)

Draw or project a picture of a mouth and a book side by side.

NOTE: Body language is often suggested as an answer to this question. Point out that body language is mostly used to assist with spoken language and cannot convey complex notions, such as your time, place, etc. There isn't a body language version of *Waiting for Godot*.

Languages are like people. They change throughout time. They also change more when they are used more.

Imagine you were given a brand new bicycle for Christmas. If you took it out every day and rode it, what changes might there be by Easter? (MUD, SCRATCHES, GENERAL WEAR AND TEAR)

Imagine that same bike at Christmas again, and this time, think what it would be like at Easter if you left it in its box that whole time and didn't use it at all. Would it have changed much? (NO)

Language is like that bike. The more you use a word, the more likely it is to change.

Our language is very old and has changed a lot over time.

But one way in which we use language has changed faster than the others because we use it much more.

Which way of using language happens more? Speaking or writing? (SPEAKING)

Draw or project an arrow downwards from the mouth to show spoken language changing. Then draw a shorter arrow downwards from the book to show written language changing.

The one we use more, speaking, changes faster. So sometimes the spelling hasn't caught up with the speaking. This is why sometimes words have letters that we no longer use and it is also why many of our old, common words have different spelling and speaking.

Let's think of some examples and write them into the word stories worksheet.

4 Word families

Neurons that fire together, wire together.

(Hebb's rule)

Most of my professional life has been spent working with children who are struggling with some aspect of language. There are times when I have had the pleasure of teaching adults too. The most memorable of these was a 79-year-old man, originally from Missouri, who walked into my practice and announced that he didn't want to go through life any more without the ability to spell.

John was raised during the Great Depression and had very little schooling to speak of, but had taught himself to read and to avoid writing so that nobody knew about his lack of education.

We did lessons once a week for an hour, and he was a keen learner, though progress was quite slow. Not only did he have deeply ingrained habits when he wrote, but I also suspected that he was in fact dyslexic. Decades of quiet determination had given him a relatively large and certainly workable sight word vocabulary, but his ability to self-correct and his knowledge of spelling conventions were really poor.

I also noticed something odd about his lexicon in general. I could successfully teach him to memorise a word like 'house' or 'like', but if a form of the word came up later, say during dictation, e.g. 'houses' or 'liked', he often couldn't spell them.

When questioned about 'houses', I distinctly remember him saying, 'But you didn't ask me to spell *house*. I can spell that, look: h-o-u-s-e.'

I asked him why he didn't just add an -s to get 'houses' and he looked at me as if I were mad. 'They're different words!' he kept insisting.

In seven decades, it had not occurred to him once that words could be altered to form new words, or indeed that any words were connected to one another except for those in wide semantic groups, such as 'mother', 'father', 'daughter', 'son'.

Research has shown that sometimes this particular understanding about words, which many of us take for granted, does not automatically occur to everyone (Ellis 1993).

Good spellers often have a highly developed sense of word-connectedness. Developing this sense is not only possible, therefore, but desirable and ultimately necessary.

An effective way to learn related facts about spelling is to analyze words by means of a word family (Nagy et al. 1989).

This chapter provides a guide to the creation of word families. This then helps students both to learn spelling patterns and to learn irregular words in connected sets.

Word families are tools to help compare and contrast words and their forms, features, or functions – in other words, what a given word is, has, or does.

Each time a word family is generated, the brain's storage and retrieval system is called upon.

Words analyzed and learned according to related characteristics help strengthen neural networks. This kind of analysis can also aid students to come to the realisation that words form a vast network, governed by a small set of predictable rules.

A word can exist in more than one family at a time, depending on the nature of the analysis. The core analytical categories are discussed here.

Form

The form is the way in which target words are spelled (or spelt).

For instance, the words 'spell' and 'tell' have the same form in the present tense. In the past tense, however, they take different forms. 'Spell' can become 'spelled', but 'tell' becomes 'told' (unless you're Scottish, and then 'telt' is acceptable too).

Therefore, an analytical focus on a family according to form would have 'spell' and 'smell' together in the same family ('spelled' and 'smelt') but 'sell' and 'tell' together in a different one ('sold' and 'told').

Feature

Words can also be related by common features. For instance, words ending with an /ee/ sound are commonly spelled with a word-final -y, not -ey (see Chapter 15: The letter <y>).

There is a set of words ending in -ey that can be learned as a separate word family.

Unlike form-related words, feature-related words don't carry meaning within their common parts, but often do share a common ancestry, which helps to explain why they are spelled as they are.

Function

Analyzing families of words according to their function is an exercise in morphology and syntax.

Function means what the word is doing in the sentence and how it relates to other words (*syntax*), that is, what part of speech it is.

Suffixes often determine function (*morphology*).

Here's an example: words ending with -ous usually denote adjectives: 'famous', 'religious', 'vicious', etc.

Words ending with -ing usually denote verbs: 'walking', 'running', 'singing'. It's up to you and your students to work out the best way of analysing and organising words for a particular family.

Word family analysis can also be used to compare and contrast homophones.

Worksheets are not necessary here; all it takes is a page in an exercise book per family. Simply write the word/words, decide on the focus, and then find other words in that family.

John helped me develop the techniques included in this chapter, and I dedicate it to his memory.

Lesson plan

Prerequisite knowledge: Can be used any time a group of words emerges.

Step 1

Turn to a blank notebook page and write the target word(s) at the top.

Step 2

Decide and write down whether your focus is the word's form, feature, or function, and write it down. Feel free to guide students with this decision until they develop an eye for it.

Step 3

Gather words and compile the family. Add new words as they come up.

Step 4

For shorter lists, you can also create sentences and stories to weave the words together. For example, to assist with the feature <eir>: 'Their heir was weird.'

TIP: Use this tool often and use plenty of examples.

Pattern to establish

Words don't exist in isolation. They can always be connected to other words through their form, feature, or function.

Error pattern

Some students see words as individual units which have to be memorised as such. This can make the idea of learning to spell understandably terrifying.

1 **Example of a word family showing common inflections**
   Form: <ought> in past tense
   Family:

Present	Past
buy	bought
bring	brought
think	thought
seek	sought
fight	fought

Accept/Except	
Accept	Except
feature: starts with ac- (to/towards)	feature: starts with ex- (out, out of)
family: access, accelerate, accord	family: extend, exit, excel

Figure 4.1 Accept/except word family

2 Example of a word family contrasting 'accept/except' (Figure 4.1)

The two target words in the families above are commonly mistaken for one another. Analysis of the feature that differentiates them, i.e. the prefix, is useful in helping students pick the right one.

Further analysis of their common feature, the base -cept-, is also useful:

Common feature: '-cept-', meaning 'take'

When you 'accept', you take in; when you 'except', you take out.

Family:

   reception, concept, intercept

3 Example of a word family showing exceptions

Feature: words ending in -ey

Words ending in an /ee/ or /i/ sound usually end in -y

Family:

   Common

      money, journey, valley, turkey, abbey, honey, jersey, jockey galley, chimney, monkey, trolley, kidney, alley, donkey, barley, storey, hockey, parsley, hackney, whiskey, blimey, crikey

   Less common

      bailey, paisley, attorney, volley, cockney, matey, joey, chutney, pulley, gurney, medley, Guernsey, odyssey, motley, gulley, cagey, bogey

4 Example of a word family showing common parts of speech

Function: adjective shown by suffix -al

   trivial, final, casual, monumental

5 Homophones

homo - same, phone - sound

A homophone is a word that sounds just like another word; the only difference is that it means something else and can be spelled differently. This can cause confusion when trying to spell the right word.

A special kind of word family can be used to help distinguish homophones. Take, for example, the word 'plane'. A plane is a flying vehicle, e.g. 'I took the plane home'.

> To work anything out in spelling, it is always a good idea to start with what you know and then look for the pattern; so it is with homophones.

Plane is also something you do to make a surface flat or smooth, e.g. 'You will need a special tool to plane that wood'.

There is also a word that sounds exactly like this but is spelled differently: 'plain', which also has several meanings:

- Not colourful or complex: 'His car was a plain white colour';
- An expanse of rural land: 'This building site used to be a plain'.

Homophones are distinct from other words that sound very similar and are commonly confused, such as 'assistants' and 'assistance'. Indeed, in some accents, these words are indistinguishable in normal speech. In this case, they are homophones.

A simple mnemonic sentence, such as 'Let's plane the plane' or 'We drove the plain car across the plain' helps group the common spellings of the homophones in memory.

To work anything out in spelling, it is always a good idea to start with what you know and then look for the pattern; so it is with homophones.

For instance: 'stationery/stationary'

A station**er** is one who provides stationery, as denoted by the suffix -er (one who does). So 'station**er**y' is the thing that is provided.

In the meantime, and perhaps with more complexity, 'station**ary'** has the -ary suffix, denoting an adjective, as in 'primary', 'secondary', 'military', and 'evolutionary'.

Explaining 'stationary' first is slightly more complex because -ary is also a noun suffix ('anniversary', 'notary', 'aviary', 'obituary', etc.). However, these nouns cannot be reduced any further by taking away the -y suffix (e.g. 'stationery/stationer') and leaving a complete word ('anniversar', 'notar', 'aviar', 'obituar'), thus providing a neat distinction between the homophones.

Looking at homophones and their common features also provides opportunities for students to make generalisations about other words.

Take 'currant/current'. The -ant ending is common in nouns ('accountant', 'antioxidant', 'hydrant', etc.) whereas the -ent ending is a common adjective suffix ('different', 'negligent', 'present') and a noun suffix in roughly equal measure ('student', 'unemployment', 'present').

Homophone study and word families can be used together to help consolidate knowledge about morphemes and suffixes.

Below is a framework for some homophone study. Then follows an alphabetical list of homophones. The list can be used in a number of ways:

- As a list that students search independently to help produce families for their chosen words;
- As a list that the teacher keeps for reference, pulling out appropriate homophones as needed;
- As a list that teacher and students go through progressively, adapting the contents somewhat for age-appropriateness. For example, most primary-school children will be able to access the difference between 'humerus/ humorous', 'lumber/lumbar', and 'pigeon/pidgin', but 'parasite/pericyte', 'insist/encyst', or 'ferrule/ferule'[1] have slightly more specialised or archaic meanings.

By all means use these words if only to highlight the fact that this generation has it considerably easier than generations past.

Lesson plan

Step 1

Pick and write down a homophone pair or group.

Step 2

Write the definition for each word.

Step 3

Note the similarities and differences.

Step 4

Compose any mnemonics to aid memory, if appropriate (see Chapter 6: Mnemonics).

---

1 *ferule* n. a flat ruler with a widened end, formerly used for beating children.

Step 5 (optional)

Create a grammatical sentence for each word.

Homophones drill

Use selected sentences from this exercise in spelling tests at the end of a homophones lesson and then at increasing time intervals (in one week, one month, etc.).

   There follows an alphabetised list of homophones. Not all accents of English will express these as homophones. Please see Appendix 1 for more information about accents.

A
ail, ale
air, heir, ere
all ready, already
allowed, aloud
assistance, assistants
attendance, attendants
awl, all

B
bail, bale
bait, bate
baize, bays
bald, balled, bawled
ball, bawl
band, banned
bar, barre
bard, barred
bare, bear
baron, barren
base, bass
based, baste
basis, basses
bask, basque
bay, bey
bazaar, bizarre
be, bee
beach, beech
beat, beet
beau, bow
been, bean, bin
beer, bier
beetle, betel
bell, belle

berg, burg
berry, bury
berth, birth
bight, bite, byte
billed, build
bird, burred
birr, burr
bit, bitt
blew, blue
bloc, block
blond, blonde
boar, bore
board, bored
boarder, border
bode, bowed
bold, bowled
bolder, boulder
bole, boll, bowl
boles, bolls, bowls
boos, booze
born, bourn, borne
bouillon, bullion
bow, bough
boy, buoy
brae, bray
braid, brayed
braise, brays, braze
brake, break
breach, breech
breaches, breeches
bread, bred
brewed, brood
brews, bruise
bridal, bridle

broach, brooch
broom, brougham
browse, brows
burger, burgher
bussed, bust
but, butt
buy, by, bye
buyer, byer

C
cache, cash
calendar, calender
calix, calyx
cannon, canon
canter, cantor
canvas, canvass
canvases, canvasses
capital, capitol
caret, carrot, karat
carol, carrel
cart, kart
cask, casque
cast, caste
caster, castor
cat'll, cattle
cause, caws
cedar, seeder
cede, seed
ceiling, sealing
cell, sell
cellar, seller
cense, cents, scents, sense
censers, censors, sensors
census, senses

cent, scent, sent
cere, sear, seer, sere
cereal, serial
cession, session
chance, chants
chard, charred
chased, chaste
cheap, cheep
check, cheque, Czech
chews, choose
chili, chilly, Chile
choral, coral
chorale, corral
chordate, cordate
chough, chuff
chucker, chukka
chute, shoot
cirrus, serous
cist, cyst
cite, sight, site
claimant, clamant
clause, claws
clew, clue
click, clique
climb, clime
close, clothes
coal, kohl
coarse, course
coat, cote
coax, cokes
cocks, cox
coffer, cougher
coin, quoin
collared, collard
colonel, kernel
complacent, complaisant
complement, compliment
concord, conquered
confectionary, confectionery
coo, coup
coop, coupe
cops, copse
coquet, coquette
cord, cored

core, corps
correspondence,
    correspondents
cosign, cosine
council, counsel
cousin, cozen
coward, cowered
crape, crepe
creak, creek
crewel, cruel
crews, cruise, cruse
crows, croze
crude, crewed
cue, queue
cues, queues
currant, current
curser, cursor
cygnet, signet
cymbal, symbol
cypress, Cyprus

D
dam, damn
Dane, deign
days, daze
dean, dene
dear, deer
deem, deme
defuse, diffuse
dense, dents
descent, dissent
dental, dentil
dependence, dependents
depravation, deprivation
descent, dissent
deviance, deviants
devisor, divisor
dew, due
die, dye
disburse, disperse
disc, disk
discreet, discrete
discussed, disgust

dissidence, dissidents
djinn, gin
doe, dough
doc, dock
doer, dour
does, doze, doughs
done, dun
dost, dust
douse, dowse
droop, drupe
dual, duel
ducked, duct
dyeing, dying

E
earn, erne, urn
eave, eve
eek, eke
eerie, eyrie
elicit, illicit
elude, allude
elusive, allusive, illusive
emerge, immerge
encyst, insist
ensure, insure
ensured, insured
epic, epoch
equivalence, equivalents
ewe, yew, you
ewer, your, you're
ewes, use, yews
exercise, exorcise
eye, aye, I
eyed, I'd
eyelet, islet

F
facts, fax
fade, fayed
fain, feign
faint, feint
fair, fare
farming, pharming

faro, pharaoh
fat, phat
fate, fete
faun, fawn
faux, foe
fay, fey
faze, phase
feat, feet
fends, fens
fiche, fish
fie, phi
filer, phylar
find, fined
fir, fur
ferule, ferrule
file, phial
filter, philtre
find, fined
firs, furs, furze
fisher, fissure
fishing, phishing
flack, flak
flacks, flax
flare, flair
flea, flee
flecks, flex
flew, flu, flue
floe, flow
florescent, fluorescent
flour, flower
flus, flues
foaled, fold
for, fore, four
forbear, forebear
foreword, forward
fort, forte
forth, fourth
foul, fowl
franc, frank
frays, phrase
frees, freeze, frieze
friar, fryer
fungous, fungus
furs, furze, firs

G

gaff, gaffe
gage, gauge
gait, gate
gamble, gambol
gays, gaze
genes, jeans
gibe, jibe
gilt, guilt
gin, jinn
graft, graphed
grate, great
grater, greater
greys, graze
greave, grieve
grill, grille
grip, grippe
grisly, grizzly
groan, grown
grocer, grosser
guessed, guest
guide, guyed
guise, guys

H

hail, hale
hair, hare
hairs, hares
hall, haul
halve, have
handsome, hansom
hangar, hanger
hart, heart
hay, hey
hays, heys, haze
heal, heel, he'll
hear, here
heard, herd
hears, here's
he'd, heed
herd, hurd
heroin, heroine
hertz, hurts

hew, hue
hi, hie, high
higher, hire
him, hymn
hoar, whore
hoard, horde
hoarse, horse
hoes, hose
hold, holed
hole, whole
holey, holy, wholly
hour, our
hours, ours
house, how's
humerus, humorous

I

idle, idyll
impassable, impassible
in, inn
incidence, incidents
incite, insight
indict, indite
innocence, innocents
iron, ion
its, it's

J

jam, jamb
jewel, joule

K

knave, nave
knead, kneed, need
kneaded, needed
kneads, needs
knew, new
knight, night
knights, nights
knit, nit
knob, nob
knot, not

know, no
knows, noes, nose

L
lacks, lax
lade, laid
lain, lane
lam, lamb
lama, llama
laps, lapse
lay, lei, ley
lea, lee
leach, leech
lead, led
leak, leek
lean, lien
leant, Lent
leas, lees
leased, least
lessen, lesson
lesser, lessor
levee, levy
levees, levies
liar, lyre
licence, license
lichen, liken
licker, liquor
lie, lye
links, lynx
lo, low
load, lode, lowed
loads, lodes
loan, lone
loaner, loner
loot, lute
luck's, lux
lumbar, lumber

M
made, maid
mail, male
main, mane
mains, manes

maize, maze
mall, maul
mandrel, mandrill
manner, manor
manners, manors
marshal, martial
martin, marten
mask, masque
mat, matte
material, materiel
mean, mien
meat, meet, mete
meatier, meteor
medal, meddle
metal, mettle
mews, muse
might, mite
millenary, millinery
mince, mints
mind, mined
miner, minor
minion, minyan
minks, minx
miscible, missable
missed, mist
misses, Mrs., missus
moan, mown
moat, mote
mode, mowed
mood, mooed
moose, mousse
mordant, mordent
morn, mourn
morning, mourning
murderess, murderous
murre, myrrh
muscle, mussel
mussed, must
mustard, mustered

N
nae, nay, neigh
naval, navel

neumatic, pneumatic
none, nun

O
oar, or, ore
ode, owed
oh, owe
one, won
oohs, ooze

P
paced, paste
packed, pact
paid, payed
pail, pale
pain, pane
pair, pare, pear
pall, pawl
pan, panne
parasite, pericyte
parlay, parley
parred, pard
passable, possible
passed, past
patience, patients
pause, paws
peace, piece
peak, peek, pique
peal, peel
pearl, purl
pedal, peddle
peer, pier
penance, pennants
pencel, pencil
per, purr
pi, pie
pic, pick
pidgin, pigeon
pistil, pistol
plain, plane
plantar, planter
pleas, please
pleural, plural

plum, plumb
pocks, pox
pole, poll
pommel, pummel
populace, populous
pore, pour, poor
practice, practise
praise, prays, preys
precedence, precedents
premier, premiere
presence, presents
presser, pressor
pride, pried
prier, prior
pries, prize
prince, prints
principal, principle
profit, prophet
pros, prose
pupal, student

Q
quarts, quartz
quean, queen
quince, quints

R
rack, wrack
raid, rayed
rain, reign, rein
raise, rays, raze,
raiser, razer, razor
rancor, ranker
rap, wrap
rapped, rapt, wrapped
rapper, wrapper
read, red
read, reed
reads, reeds
real, reel
recite, resite
reek, wreak
resister, resistor

rest, wrest
retch, wretch
review, revue
rheumy, roomy
rigger, rigor
right, rite, wright, write
rime, rhyme
ring, wring
ringers, wringers
rise, ryes
road, rode, rowed
roe, row
role, roll
root, route
rose, rows
rote, wrote
rued, rude
rues, ruse
rum, rhumb
rung, wrung
rye, wry

S
sac, sack
sachet, sashay
sacks, sax
sail, sale
sane, Seine
scene, seen
scull, skull
sea, see, cee
seal, seel
seam, seem
seamed, seemed
seamen, semen
sear, seer, sere, cere
seas, sees, seize
sects, sex
senate, sennit, sennet
serf, surf
serge, surge
settler, settlor
sew, so, sow

sewer, suer
sews, sows
sexed, sext
sextan, sexton
shear, sheer
sheave, shiv
shoe, shoo
shone, shown
sic, sick
side, sighed
sighs, size
sign, sine, syne
signet, cygnet
sink, sync
sinking, syncing
slay, sleigh
sleight, slight
slew, slough
soar, sore
sole, soul
some, sum
son, sun, sunn
sonny, sunny
sou, sue
source, sauce
spade, spayed
specks, specs
spits, spitz
spoor, spore
stade, staid, stayed
staff, staph
stair, stare
stairs, stares
stake, steak
stanch, staunch
stationary, stationery
steal, steel
step, Steppe
sticks, Styx
stile, style
strait, straight
succour, sucker
suede, swayed
suite, sweet

sundae, Sunday
surplice, surplus

T
tacked, tact,
tacks, tax
tail, tale
taper, tapir
tare, tear
taught, tot, taut
tea, tee
team, teem
tear, tier
teas, tease, tees
tense, tents
tern, turn
Thai, tie
their, there, they're
theirs, there's
threw, through
throe, throw
throne, thrown
tic, tick
tied, tide
tighten, titan
'til, till
timber, timbre
timbers, timbers
time, thyme
tire, tyre

to, too, two
toad, toed, towed
toe, tow
told, tolled
tole, toll
ton, tun
toughed, tuft
tracked, tract
tracks, tracts
trade, trayed
tray, trey
troop, troupe
troops, troupes
trussed, trust
tuna, tuner
twill, 'twill

V

vail, vale, veil
vain, vane, vein
vales, veils
vial, vile, viol
vice, vise
villain, villein

W
wade, weighed
wail, wale, whale
wain, wane
waist, waste

wait, weight
waive, wave
waiver, waver
want, wont
war, wore
ward, warred
ware, wear, where
warn, worn
wart, wort
way, weigh
we, wee
weed, we'd
weak, week
weakly, weekly
weal, we'll, wheel
wean, ween
weather, wether, whether
weave, we've
weighs, ways
we're, weir
wheal, wheel
who's, whose
wind, wined, whined
wood, would

Y
yoke, yolk
you'll, Yule
you're, yore, your

6 Mnemonics

Paying attention to a word's structure and story when introducing new words is important, but there are times when extra memory resources have to be employed to make them stick. This is where mnemonics come in.

Mnemonics can be, amongst many things, acronyms, songs, jingles, rhymes, stories, or catchphrases.

Mnemonics work well because they employ some or all of four major formats of representation that the brain uses:

1 visual
2 phonological
3 grammatical
4 mentalese, 'the language of thought in which our conceptual knowledge is couched' (Pinker 1997)

This applies even in a simple sentence like 'Only Crabs' Eyes Are Narrow' to remember the spelling of the word 'ocean'.

The sentence can easily be associated with a mental picture of the ocean or anything else that will help set the context. It organises the initial letters in a way that aids recall. It makes sense, and thinking about it, working out each letter, focuses the attention on the facts to be recalled, strengthening the pathway.

Necessary

Not Every Cat Eats Sardines – Some Are Really Yummy. Don't forget that the cat has one collar and two socks (one <c> and two <s>s).

Cemetery

Three <e>s are buried in the cemetery.

ow/ou

These two digraphs, their sounds, spellings, and example words are often hard to learn for young children and struggling spellers, so this is the story we tell at the practice:

There was once a kind farmer who let his animals come into his house and warm themselves by the fire in winter.

One day the farmer had been working in the fields and was tired and cold. His feet were sore and his head ached. He came into his house only to be confronted by a large cow standing by the fire. He politely tried to find a space so that he could get warm, but the cow only pushed him further from the heat, and in doing so stepped on his foot.

That was the last straw! The farmer lost his patience and shouted at the top of his voice, 'Ow! Out of the house now, cow!'

Practice/practise

The word 'ice' is a noun, and the word 'is' is a verb, corresponding to the noun/verb distinction in the two words. American English no longer makes this distinction.

The <c> = noun/<s> = verb distinction can also be expanded to explain 'licence/license', 'advice/advise', 'device/devise'.

Inquiry/enquiry

Inquiry: Link to the <i> in 'investigation'. 'We will mount an INquiry.'

Enquiry: Link to the <e> in 'request'. 'May I enquire as to how long you'll be?'

Conscience

That thing in your mind that lets you *know* right from wrong.

It comes from Latin. The Latin base word in 'conscience' is 'scio' (pronounced /skee-o/), which means 'I know'. This is where we get 'science' from, a far easier word to spell because it is common and we hear the <s> clearly.

Science is about knowledge, and the prefix 'con-' means 'with'. So when you do something *with knowledge* of right and wrong, you use your conscience:

con + science

there/they're/their

The first two are simple to explain, though the last one is a little trickier.

Start with 'there': This tells us the location. It has the word 'here' in it, just like the location word 'where'.

So you could have the following dialogue:

'Where? Here?!'
'No! There!'

Then explain that 'they're' is a contraction, short for 'they are'. So you must spell the word 'they' first.

Then you can explain that 'their' means that 'they' own something. The first three letters of 'their' and 'they' are the same. The <y> becomes <i>, as it usually does when it stops being at the end of a word (see Chapter 25: The return of Illegal <i>). The letter <r> is added to show belonging, just like in 'her'.

So the pattern goes: they + r = their
                             their - r = they

---

two/too/to

Although it is not recommended to teach these homophones all at once, as this presents too much of a cognitive load to novices, the lesson below illustrates the difference between the three words and offers ways of mapping and recalling them.

- two dialogue (answers in brackets):

How many people are there in a set of TWins? (TWo)
  How many times is something done when it's done TWice? (TWo)
  How much is ten times TWo? (TWenty)
  What is ten plus TWo? (TWelve)
  So, words that have something to do with the number two have the letters 'tw' at the beginning. It's just that you don't hear the <w> in the actual number, but you have to remember to write it.

- 'too': There are TOOOOOOOOOO many os in the TOO of quantity. And when you leave a dog behind, he howls, 'Take me TOOOOOOOO!'
- 'to': Though I tend not to use the terms 'short' and 'long' for sounds (Chapter 14), I find that it does help to explain that this version of the homophone is often unstressed in sentences. This causes us to schwa the vowel (see Chapter 23: Schwa). In other words, we often use the short version of this word and we spell it short. Contrasted with 'too', which we normally stress when speaking, it feels natural to shorten the short version and lengthen the long version. Compare the sentences:
'We walked to Longacre.'
'We walked too long.'
Try lengthening the /oo/ in 'to' in the first sentence: 'We walked toooooo Longacre'.
Now try shortening the /oo/ in 'too' in the second sentence: 'We walked t'long'.
How does that feel?

7 Counting syllables

What is a syllable?

A syllable can be defined as an uninterrupted unit of sound that can be made with one impulse of the voice. For example, the word 'window', if hummed rather than said, requires your vocal cords to make two separate humming sounds. Try it and see.

This chapter is a guide to a quick, 5-minute game of syllable counting that can be used at the start of each spelling lesson until students can reliably count syllables in words.

Many of the example words generated in the first few lessons are one-syllable words. Everyday language, of course, even at the pre-school level, contains countless polysyllablic words. Syllable awareness, therefore, is an important foundational skill for literacy.

To ensure that students are syllable-aware, we need to examine ways of counting them that will work for each individual.

A syllable can be defined as an uninterrupted unit of sound that can be made with one impulse of the voice.

This is a relatively short lesson, and one that can be used at any time if the concept of syllables is unfamiliar.

Three sensory pathways

There are three sensory pathways that we can use in order to count syllables in words:

1 Auditory

  The first is through the ears, the auditory pathway. Students can be asked to count the number of syllables that they *hear*, and indeed, many can reliably give the correct answer.

2 Kinaesthetic

  We can increase sensory input by adding kinaesthetic cues to the process. Students often nod their heads or clap for each syllable.

3   Visual

Third, and most effectively for anyone with working memory issues, students can be asked to point one finger for every syllable that they hear/feel. At the end of the word, they can count the pointed fingers. Now they can see the number of syllables too.

Naturally, using all three sensory pathways to count syllables increases reliability.

Here are some techniques incorporating one or more of the pathways:

Jaw-dropping

By nature of their production, vowels require some degree of opening in the vocal tract (see Chapter 10: The difference between vowels and consonants).

An extreme example is the sound /u/ as in 'cut', where the tract is fully open. Contrast this with the sound /ee/ as in 'keep', and you can feel your jaw rising as you alternate the sounds.

Your students can therefore place their hands underneath their chins whilst carefully saying the target word and counting how many 'jaw drops' occur.

Desk thumping

Have students bang a closed fist on their desk for every syllable in the target word. Don't forget to have them point a finger for every thump.

Line dancing

Have five students stand at the front of the class and get each one to STEP and remain forward for each syllable in the target word.

Nose impulses

Have students close their lips tight and say the target word. All the air escapes through the nose in distinct impulses.

Syllable counting for reading

When reading, syllables can be counted by underlining and counting the single vowels and vowel digraphs. There is a one-to-one match between number of vowels and number of syllables. Final Silent E is not counted (see Chapter 16: Final Silent E).

Example:
misunderstood   Four lines, four syllables ('er' and 'oo' are digraphs, Chapter 21)
investigate   Four lines, four syllables (Final Silent E not counted, Chapter 16)

Lesson plan

Skill level

Any

Pattern

For every syllable there is a vowel sound.

Error pattern

Confusing phonemes with syllables is often done at first. For example, the word 'wanted' is sounded out /w-a-n-t-ed/ and the answer 'five syllables' is given. In this instance, students can be asked to hum the word quickly, as in normal speech, and count the impulses. Always go back to de-emphasising the separate phonemes when this occurs.

Duration

5 minutes at the start of each spelling lesson until students can reliably count syllables.

Step 1

Choose your counting method.

Step 2

Say words of between two and five syllables and have students count them.

TIP: Start with students' first names and surnames so that each person gets a chance to participate.

A list of between two and five-syllable words is presented for easy reference (Figure 7.1). In some cases, syllables collapse into one another at certain boundaries, rendering the word a whole syllable short. Words like this are indicated by an alternative number in brackets, e.g. 'nobody' (2): some people will say /no-bud-ee/ and some will say /no-bdee/.

2 syllables		3 syllables		4 syllables		5 syllables	
about	water	addition	relative	application	stationary	accommodation	satisfactory
across	winter	afternoon	remember	atmospheric	stationery	antagonistic	similarity
after	without	animal	represent	available	television	appreciative	specifically
alone	yellow	another	Saturday	calculation	testimony	argumentative	superintendent
along		anything		celebration		association	
apple		anyway		ceremony		characteristic	
around		beautiful		circumference		civilization	
author		beginning		colonial		communication	
baby		company		combination		consideration	
became		connection		community		continuation	
become		December		companionship		conversational	
behind		department		comparison		curiosity	
belong		direction		conventional		decomposition	
better		election		dictionary		determination	
between		employment		difficulty		dramatically	
brother		everything		disagreement		electricity	
cannot		family		discovery		elementary	
cover		gentleman		distribution		environmental	
delay		history		education		equatorial	
dinner		holiday		elaborate		eventually	
even		however		entertainment		examination	
female		important		establishment		experimental	
finish		nautical		everybody		familiarity	
forget		newspaper		exceptional		horizontally	
forgot		nobody		experience		imagination	
Friday		November		favourable		immediately	
happy		objection		generally		inactivity	
inside		October		identify		indigestible	
letter		officer		illustration		individual	
maybe		passenger		impossible		investigation	
Monday		permission		imprisonment		manufacturing	
never		personal		inheritance		miscellaneous	
only		position		interference		observatory	
other		president		investigate		occasionally	
outside		primary		January		oppositional	
paper		property		material		ordinarily	
party		regular		necessary		organisation	
report		September		particular		originated	
river		several		political		perpendicular	
seven		computer		population		personality	
sister		understand		publication		popularity	
Sunday		estimate		respectfully		preliminary	
supper		telephone		responsible		relationship	
today		director		understanding		university	
twenty		confusion		unfortunate		unprofessional	
under		violin		vegetable		victoriously	

Figure 7.1 Polysyllable wordlist

8 Affixes

Competent, mature readers and spellers (as opposed to struggling or emerging ones) rely on their ability to break longer words down into easily manageable parts. They have some knowledge of the rules of syllable division. They have a working vocabulary of prefixes and suffixes (known collectively as *affixes*). They know and understand a good number of base elements too. Their lexicon is now much more sensitive to the structure and content of word forms (*morphology*).

They can make accurate predictions regarding how a word they have never seen before should be spelled or pronounced and can deduce meanings by understanding various word-parts.

This chapter is a basic introduction to morphology as it applies to spelling. In the lessons, we will work from a list of nine prefixes, nine suffixes, and nine bases. This list is by no means exhaustive or exclusive of any other list.

> By fourth grade, most average students are generalising their knowledge of prefixes, suffixes and bases to decipher the meanings of hundreds of new words encountered in reading.
>
> Moats (1995)

Prefixes

un-, re-, de-, pre-, pro-, con-, com-, ex-, sub-

Suffixes

-ly, -al, -ship, -er (one who does), -er (more), -ful, -ed, -est, -ist

Base elements

These are a little trickier, as they are often more heavily embedded within words and tend to change around the edges, depending on their environment.

Uncertainty about bases is also common if the following isn't known and understood: There are two types of base element:

1 Unbound – those which are words on their own (e.g. 'play' in 'replay', 'do' in 'undo')
2 Bound – those which cannot stand alone and must have a prefix or a suffix added (e.g. '-ject-' in 'project', 'reject'; '-plex-' in 'complex', 'duplex')

Our list of bases is:

hope, sense, view, -ject-, quick, walk, -plex-, wide, -duc-

Lesson plan

Skill level

- Handwriting
- Phonic skills to the polysyllable level
- Knowledge of the parts of speech (optional but handy for suffixes)

Materials

- Prefix, suffix, and base element worksheets (Figures 8.2, 8.4, 8.6)
- Dictionary

Prefix	Definition	Examples
un-	not	unable, unhappy
re-	back, again	return, replay
de-	down, away from	depend, defend
pre-	before	prefix, prepare
pro-	in front of, for	produce, protect
con-	with, together	contrast, confidence
com-	with, together	company, committee
ex-	out, away from	exit, extension
sub-	under	subway, submarine

> **RULE:** When reading and spelling long words, look out for prefixes.

Figure 8.1 Prefix completed worksheet

Prefix	Definition	Examples
un-		
re-		
de-		
pre-		
pro-		
con-		
com-		
ex-		
sub-		

RULE:

Figure 8.2 Prefix blank worksheet

Suffix	Definition	Examples	Part of speech
-ly	in a certain manner	ably, happily	adverb
-al	associated with, like	final, comical	adjective
-ship	to do with status, how something is	friendship, hardship	noun
-er	one who does	carer, trader	noun
-er	more	bigger, shorter	adjective
-ful	having qualities of	beautiful	adjective
-ed	in the past	painted, complained	verb
-est	most	tallest, kindest	adjective
-ist	one who does	artist, dentist	noun

> **RULE:** When reading and spelling long words, look out for suffixes.

Figure 8.3 Suffix completed worksheet

Duration

5 minutes per affix

Step 1

If not already known, introduce the concept of prefixes with the word 'undo', drawing attention to un- and asking for other un- words.

Step 2

Distribute the prefix worksheet (Figure 8.2) and work through the suggested prefixes. You can also work on prefixes of your own choosing. The list here is a suggestion only.

NOTE: The prefixes con- and com- mean the same thing. As an extension exercise, your students can figure out where to use con- vs. com-. The answer is all about the base. If the pronunciation of the base ends at the front of the mouth – /b, m, p/ – then com- is much easier to say. Contrast 'combustion/conbustion', 'communicate/conmunicate', 'compliance/conpliance'.

Step 3

Write down the rule:

When reading and spelling long words, look out for prefixes.

Suffix	Definition	Examples	Part of speech
-ly			
-al			
-ship			
-er			
-er			
-ful			
-ed			
-est			
-ist			

RULE:

Figure 8.4 Suffix blank worksheet

Word	Prefix	Base	Suffix
hopeless	-	hope	-less
unable	un-	able	-
reviewer	re-	view	-er
inject	in-	-ject-	
quickly	-	quick	-ly
walking	-	walk	-ing
complexity	com-	-plex-	-ity
widen	-	wide	-en
uninterested	un-	interest	-ed

Bases carry the main meaning of words.

Figure 8.5 Base element example worksheet

Step 4

Repeat with suffixes but this time draw attention to the fact that suffixes often show the part of speech a word is. If the concept of parts of speech is unfamiliar, it is best to pre-teach these. You can simplify things by not mentioning the connection between suffixes and parts of speech and letting your students work out the common function of the words they use as examples.

Step 5

Write down the rule:

When reading and spelling long words, look out for suffixes.

Step 6

Repeat for base elements, making sure to point out the difference between a bound and unbound base.

Step 7

Write down the definition:

Base elements carry the main meaning of words.

Word	Prefix	Base	Suffix
hopeless			
unable			
reviewer			
inject			
quickly			
walking			
complexity			
widen			
uninterested			

Figure 8.6 Base element blank worksheet

Example lesson: Prefixes

> Write the word 'undo' on the board.

What word? ('UNDO')

How many syllables? (TWO)

One of the best ways to break words down is to look for familiar parts, that is, parts that you've seen or heard in other words. In the word 'undo', have you seen the beginning of that word before? (YES, UN-)

Un- is a common beginning. The name we will use for a common beginning is *prefix*. You see this prefix at the beginning of lots of words in English.

Can you think of any more words with more than one syllable that begin with un-?

To show that we have found a prefix, we will underline the whole prefix:

<u>un</u>do

When spelling this word, if you already know what the prefix is, now you really only have to deal with the sounds in one syllable instead of two.

Write this in the rule box on your worksheet.

RULE: When reading and spelling long words, look out for prefixes.

We are now going to look at a list of prefixes and come up with a definition and examples for each one. Write them on your worksheet and put a hyphen straight after them to show that there is at least one syllable to follow:

un-, re-, de-, pre-, pro-, con-, com-, ex-, sub-

Example lesson: Suffixes

Our next word is 'repeated'.

There are three syllables in this word.

Now let's look for familiar parts, that is, parts that you've seen or heard in other words.

In the word 'repeated', have you seen the beginning of that word before? (YES, RE-)

Re- is a prefix. It means 'back' or 'again'. You see this prefix at the beginning of lots of words in English.

Can you think of any more words that begin with re-?

There is also a common ending on this word. Do you know what it is? (-ED)

-ed is used at the end of many words in English to show past tense. The name for a common ending is *suffix*.

Can you think of any more words with the suffix -ed?

Now you actually only have one syllable left to deal with, making the word much easier to work out.

What syllable? (THE MIDDLE ONE, SPELLED 'P-E-A-T')

Let's write the rule:

RULE: When reading and spelling long words, look out for suffixes.

We are now going to look at a list of suffixes and come up with a definition and examples for each one. Write them on your worksheet and put a hyphen straight before to show that there is at least one syllable before it:

-ly, -al, -ship, -er (one who does), -er (more), -ful, -ed, -est, -ist

There are two suffixes that are spelled the same but mean different things, the suffixes -er. We will put their meanings in brackets.

Fill in the prefix and suffix worksheets before tackling bases.

Example lesson: Bases

All those prefixes and suffixes wouldn't have any work to do if we couldn't add them to what we call *bases*.

Bases are like the heads of families. They carry the main meaning of words. We add prefixes and suffixes to adjust the meaning.

For example, the word 'painfully' can be broken down, or reduced, by taking off the suffix -ly.

What word is left? ('PAINFUL')

Can we break the word down any more? (YES, BY REMOVING THE SUFFIX -FUL)

What word is left? ('PAIN')

Can this be reduced any further? (NO)

Could we add any other suffixes to the base 'pain'? (YES, -ED OR -LESS, FOR EXAMPLE)

There are two kinds of base, those that are words on their own and those that are not words unless a prefix and/or suffix is added to them.

If we take the word 'play', it's the base for the word 'replay'. Is 'play' a word on its own? (YES)

'Replay' is a different word. How is it different? (WE ADDED THE PREFIX RE- AND THE NEW WORD NOW MEANS TO PLAY AGAIN)

Do the words 'play' and 'replay' have different meanings? (YES, BUT THEY ARE VERY CLOSE IN MEANING.)

So that's how a prefix can change a base that stands on its own as a word.

Now let's consider a word like 'reject'. What is the prefix? (RE-)

What does that make the base? (-JECT-)

Is that a word on its own? (NO)

It's a base meaning 'to throw'. We see -ject- in lots of words. Can you think of other words with the base -ject-? ('INJECT', 'SUBJECT', 'CONJECTURE')

The base contains the basic meaning of the word, which remains the same even though the overall meaning of the word can be changed by prefixes and suffixes.

Let's write that and figure out all the prefixes, bases, and suffixes in the next worksheet.

Affixes spelling drill

1   unlikely
2   between
3   remember
4   produce
5   developed
6   result
7   control
8   expect
9   prepared
10   direction
11   predict
12   completely
13   access
14   ownership
15   shouted
16   subway
17   rejection
18   beautiful
19   hopefully
20   biggest

9 The Spelling Formula

Formula: A method or procedure for achieving something.

(The Oxford English Dictionary 1989)

The Spelling Formula is a self-checking, self-correcting mechanism that can be used to analyze and spell words of more than one syllable.

This formula reinforces our innate understanding that 'phonological rules apply in an ordered sequence' (Pinker 1994). Using the sequential steps of the formula helps demystify the task of spelling polysyllablic words.

It is worth noting at this point that students won't have to labour over the steps in the formula for the rest of their lives (a relief to many). Going through the steps is simply a process whereby they can replace or avoid faulty mechanisms and, instead, use something a little closer to the process competent spellers actually employ.

The point at which you introduce The Spelling Formula is a matter for your judgement, though handwriting and basic phonics skills, including syllable awareness, are a must.

There will be times when the formula doesn't generate the target word on a 1:1 basis. For instance, a student might come up with 'krizanthamem' for 'chrysanthemum', but in cases like this, the analysis and sequencing are still valuable and the solution opens the door to further analysis along etymological lines (i.e. Greek root so <ch> and <y>; -anther is a flower part, etc.).

Spelling is subject to sets of rules. A correctly spelled word is an observable phenomenon, in much the same way as a mathematical equation is. On that basis, The Spelling Formula allows students to work through a series of testable hypotheses to derive a solution.

NOTE for intervention teachers: If you are working with one or a small group of intervention students, please make sure that they do not skip any of the steps for at least ten words in a row. As you probably know, a common coping strategy of those who have difficulty spelling is to rush ahead and skip steps. This gives the impression that the learner is processing the language tasks as quickly as those who aren't struggling. It keeps them from being noticed. Insist that all steps are done, in sequence, for at least ten words.

> Spelling is subject to sets of rules. A correctly spelled word is an observable phenomenon, in much the same way as a mathematical equation is.

Lesson plan

Skill level

- Chapter 7: Counting syllables
- Handwriting
- Knowledge of the sound-letter correspondences of the alphabet

Materials

- Figure 9.1

Patterns

- All syllables must contain a vowel.
- The weak vowel is most likely to be 'a/e', followed by ‹i›, ‹o›, and then ‹u›.
- 'Keeping it simple' gives better results.

Duration

30 minutes for the introduction, 3–5 minutes per word.

Step 1

Count syllables.

Distribute The Spelling Formula flow chart (Figure 9.1). Start by choosing and saying clearly the target word and asking your students to count the syllables. To demonstrate the process, we will use the target word 'demonstrate'.

Step 2

Draw lines.

On a working-out page, students draw three horizontal lines, one for each syllable:

—— —— ——

Step 3

Start with what I know.

Depending on the word, this could mean that there is a recognizable affix, such as un- or -ing. Alternatively, if you are using the formula to help generate examples of other word features, such as consonant + le endings or a particular vowel digraph, you can start by putting what is known on the appropriate syllable line. Sometimes the only thing readily known is the initial letter. Start there by all means.

Before writing the initial letter, students should get into the habit of saying the whole syllable as best they can. With 'demonstrate', some will say ‹de›, others will say ‹dem›. What we are looking for is the ability to say the sounds in sequence. Knowledge about syllable division is a higher-order skill and not the focus of this lesson.

Students write that first syllable on the first line and do the next step, following the flow chart.

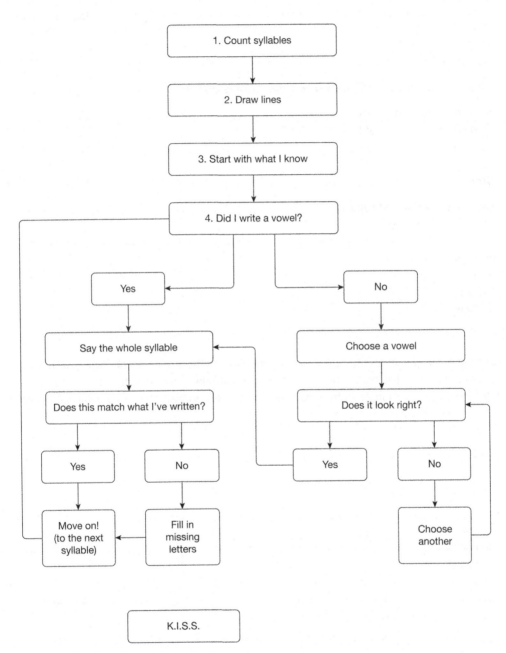

Figure 9.1 Spelling Formula flow chart

Step 4

Did I write a vowel?

YES.

Morphologically speaking, the first syllable ends at the vowel. So far, the syllable lines look like this:

de ___ ___

Step 5 (and return to Step 4 when this step is done)

Say the whole syllable: 'DE'

Does this match what I've written? YES.

Move on!

Step 6

Say and write the next syllable.

Possible answers:

de man __
de men __
de min __
de mon __
de mun __

Choose which one 'looks right'. You may just have to tell the students. This is okay. If they are capable of understanding, it is always good to point out the meaning of the base and examine other words in that family. In this case, the bound base -monst- means 'to point out, show'. We also have *monster* in this family!

Step 7

Say and write the next syllable.

Possible answers:

de mon straight
de mon strait
de mon strate

Choose which one is the simplest, most common option ('strate'). You may just have to tell the students. This is okay.

Step 8

Write the whole word.

Notes

Syllable emphasis and your mental lexicon

Because the middle syllable in 'demonstrate' is unstressed (i.e. emphasis is on the first syllable), the vowel within it is unclear.

You may well think that the letter <o> is highly apparent, but that is because the word 'demonstrate', in all likelihood, is fully formed in your mental lexicon. When you think of this word, your mind brings up a sound and a picture (as well as other mental representations to do with meaning, origin, etc.).

An unfamiliar word would offer you much less information, especially the vowel inside an unstressed syllable. For example, is it 'collectable' or 'collectible'?

In fact, it's both, but it serves to demonstrate the fact that it is often impossible to determine the vowel sound in an unstressed syllable based on auditory information alone.

Simply because you might have a multi-sensory mental representation for a word doesn't mean your students do.

This indeterminate vowel sound in unstressed syllables is known as *schwa* (Chapter 23).

For now, though, your students need to know that if they can't clearly hear the vowel, then they most likely have a choice of six single letters. In descending order of commonality, they are:

a, e (roughly equal)

i

o

u

y

The trap of over-pronunciation

As teachers, we are keen to help our students succeed. We can, as a result, fall into the trap of over-pronouncing the target word. We sometimes try to give phonemic clues by making the vowels in unstressed syllables very clear in spelling lessons and even in assessments. This over-pronunciation does not reflect natural conversation and so is limiting in its usefulness. Furthermore, if you clearly enunciate the unstressed vowel, whose brain is doing the work?

That is not to discourage anyone from providing the missing letters once students have had enough attempts, but using *your* brain to come up with the unstressed vowel rather than *theirs* denies them a valuable learning opportunity.

Process of elimination, prior knowledge, or finally just plain teacher help brings us to these syllables:

de mon strate

Example lesson

Distribute The Spelling Formula flow chart (Figure 9.1) and explain that the students will be using this to work out what to do when figuring out longer words in spelling.
  Target word: 'complicated'
  Students

- count syllables (4);
- draw lines;
- start with what they know, perhaps the prefix 'com-' and the suffix '-ed'.

Move on to syllable two.
  Did I write a vowel?
  No? Choose a vowel.
  The vowel in this syllable is unclear because it is in a weak syllable. Students must choose from <a>, <e>, <i>, <o>, or <u> and figure out what looks right.

Now we need to find the vowel. The problem is, this is a weak syllable, and the sound of the vowel is not very clear. Do you know what our most likely choices are when we're looking for a vowel in a weak syllable? (THE SINGLE VOWELS <A>, <E>, <I>, <O>, and <U>)

NOTE: It is these single vowels that appear as the vowels in weak syllables significantly more than anything else. Keep it simple by trying these first.

Which one looks right? (I)
  Write it on the second line.

  com i __ ed

You've written a vowel. Now say the whole syllable again. Does it match what you've written? (NO)
  Then fill in the missing letters and move on.

  com pli __ ed

Next syllable. What vowel? (/A/)
  It's easy to hear that vowel because it's in the strong syllable. How do you think we should spell it? (<A>)
  Why not <ay>, or <ai>? (THAT WOULDN'T BE KEEPING IT SIMPLE)

But vowels don't say their name for no reason. Why would this vowel be saying its name? (BECAUSE IT'S AT THE END OF A SYLLABLE)

Okay, so our vowel is <a>. Write it in, say the syllable, and fill in the missing letters. Now you have your word. Write it out as a complete word.

The next example is a trickier word that requires a little more teacher input. There are times when you will have to simply tell the students the answer. The point of this exercise is to demonstrate a process.

Target word: 'absquatulated'

Let's assume we've defined the word, counted the syllables, and drawn five lines.

What is Step 3? (START WITH WHAT YOU KNOW. WE KNOW THAT THE SUFFIX IS -ED AND THE PREFIX IS AB-)

ab ___ ___ ___ ed

Let's start after the prefix and say the whole second syllable.

What does the second syllable sound like? ('SQUAT')

How do we write that?

ab squat ___ ___ ed

What does the third syllable sound like? ('YOU')

NOTE: Some students will want to write 'you' for this syllable. This is where you bring in that important concept called 'Keep It Simple, Students (K.I.S.S.)' again. Here's how …

When you hear the sound /ue/ in a word, the best thing to try is a single letter. What letter? (<U>)

That's right. You could also use the letters <ue> or even <you> together. But what I want you to remember is that you will be right most often if you keep it simple.

The first part of keeping it simple is that you should try to use the most common letter or letters for a sound. In English words, the most common letter for the /ue/ sound is the letter <u>, especially if it's at the end of a syllable.

The second part of keeping it simple is to use one letter instead of two wherever you possibly can.

So to revise the 'Keep It Simple' principle:

• Use the most common letter.
• Use one letter instead of two.

You will be right most often if you stick to 'Keep It Simple.'

So getting back to the syllable /u/. How would you spell it? (<U>)

ab squat u ___ ed

Now that you've done all the steps, you need to cycle back through the steps again until you've figured out the whole word.

So, Step 4? (HAVE YOU WRITTEN A VOWEL? NO: CHOOSE A VOWEL.)

What vowel? (<A>)

Write it on line four. Can we leave this syllable with just one letter? (NO, THERE'S MORE: AN <L>)

ab squat u la ed

What consonant comes next? (T)

The word without the -ed suffix is 'absquatulate'. The <t> before Final Silent E can arguably stay in that syllable after adding the suffix, which follows a morphological pattern, or it can be transferred to the final syllable, thus giving us a signal to continue pronouncing the <a> as its name since it is an open syllable. The two alternatives are below:

ab squat u lat ed

or

ab squat u la ted

As you can see, there is quite a rhythm that can be generated here.

It may seem like a lot of slow work at first, especially if there are some students in your class who already know how to spell the words and want to skip steps. However, your focus is on having all your students able to use and then internalise this strategy, so ask the higher spellers to be patient and try to elicit answers from those who don't already know the words.

The following is one more example, showing how the questioning process can be sped up once students start to grasp the steps.

Target word: 'unlawfully'

> Step 1? (COUNT THE SYLLABLES, THERE ARE FOUR)
>   Step 2? (DRAW LINES)
>
> ___ ___ ___ ___
>
> Step 3? (START WITH WHAT YOU KNOW: WE KNOW THAT THE PREFIX IS 'UN-')
>
> <u>un</u> ___ ___ ___
>
> Write it on the prefix line. What else? (THE SUFFIXES ARE -FUL AND -LY)
>
> <u>un</u> ___ <u>ful</u> <u>ly</u>
>
> Write them on the suffix lines.
>   There's not much else to figure out here. Say the whole missing syllable. ('LAW')
>   This is the base element. How do you spell it? (<L-A-W>)
>   Write it in and write the whole word out.

What to do if The Spelling Formula doesn't generate all the letters in the target word

1 Don't panic!
2 Use word-referencing if you can. This is a method of getting your students to think of other words in the target word's family. For example, if you're looking for the vowel in the second syllable in the word 'confidence', you get a clue by thinking of the vowel in the second syllable of the word 'confide'. The vowel sound is now very clear. The same can be said for 'generate/generic', 'commend/commendation', etc.
3 Understand that once they have had a fair attempt, it's okay to guide your students through a word by simply telling them the letters they need.
4 Remember that you are *practising* a formula that will help them internalise a good strategy for spelling. Sometimes they will simply have to look the word up (as we all do).
5 Have your students understand that with The Spelling Formula, they will be much closer to the target word than if they just guessed. This will make readers more able to understand what they meant. This will also make it easier to find the word in a dictionary.

10 The difference between vowels and consonants

The purpose of this chapter is

- to teach students the difference between vowels and consonants;
- to get them to understand why we must have a vowel sound in every syllable of every word in English.

So often, the terms *vowel* and *consonant* are used in spelling instruction, but a student's understanding often goes no further than being able to name which letters of the alphabet belong to which category. They have no idea what makes a vowel a vowel and a consonant a consonant. Research shows that having that basic linguistic knowledge is often an advantage (Lindamood and Lindamood 1998).

The difference between vowels and consonants is simply this:

- Consonants can be voiced or unvoiced and are made by obstructing the passage of your breath in some way.
- Vowels are always voiced and are made by not blocking your breath. They come out freely, as if you are singing.

The shape of your mouth and the position of your jaw and tongue vary from vowel to vowel, but each sound comes out with no obstruction.

Vowels are like musical notes. They carry the greatest amount of acoustic information in syllables. Test this out by trying to sing 'Do Re Mi Fa So La Ti Do' without the vowels!

The difference between vowels and consonants is simply this:

- Consonants can be voiced or unvoiced and are made by obstructing the passage of your breath in some way.
- Vowels are always voiced and are made by not blocking your breath. They come out freely, as if you are singing.

Lesson plan

Skill level

Any. No reading or writing is required. These principles are fundamental to literacy, and because they require no reading or writing, can be taught from pre-school onwards.

Materials

To assist your students to get a full, conceptual understanding of the difference between vowels and consonants, it helps to demonstrate how we use our body to make speech sounds.

By discovering, then drawing/projecting the human articulatory mechanism and moving various letters through this, your students notice the way vowels and consonants feel, and in doing so, they can determine their differences.

You will also need some magnetic letters, both vowels and consonants.

Duration

30 minutes.

Step 1

Start by asking your students to come up with the different parts of the articulatory mechanism (the machine that humans use to make speech sounds). You will end up drawing or projecting a picture of the lungs, trachea, throat, tongue, teeth, and lips on the board. It doesn't have to be anatomically perfect; you just have to get the idea of these body parts across to the students (see Figure 10.1).

Step 2

Confirm which are the moving, sound-producing parts (the articulators). These are the tongue, the moving jaw, and the lips.

This can be done by having students try to say their names without first moving their tongues, then without their jaws, then without their lips.

Step 3

Show how /p/ is articulated by moving the magnetic letter <p> through the hollow tube starting in the lungs and moving into the mouth. Discover which articulators are moving (the lips) and focus particularly on the fact that the passage of the air was blocked by the two lips coming together, forcing the air to push its way past in order to make the sound.

Example questions:

- Is the air obstructed or unobstructed?
- Did the air come out freely, or did you have to make some effort to get it out?
- Did something get in the way?
- Was there something momentarily stopping that air from coming out?
- Did it have to push its way out?

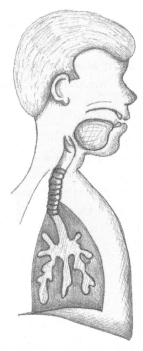

Figure 10.1 The human articulatory mechanism

Step 4

Once students have grasped the fact that there was obstruction there, they can be told that when the air has to force, push, or get through a narrow opening whilst causing friction (e.g. /s/), then that is a consonant.

Step 5

Try other consonants using Figures 10.2 and 10.3.

Step 6

Choose the vowel /a/ as in 'cat'. Show the path the air takes by moving a magnetic letter <a> from the lungs and through the hollow tube. When the air reaches the mouth, ask students to feel and describe how the air leaves the mouth.

This time the example questions will result in different answers. Once students have grasped that the production of /a/ occurs without obstruction, they can be told that when the air doesn't have to force, push, or get through a narrow opening with friction, then that is a vowel.

Step 7

Try other vowels to reinforce this concept. Figure 10.4 is a simple guide to vowel production.

Unvoiced	Voiced	Construction
p (pig)	b (big)	The air comes from the lungs and is stopped by the lips before coming out in a popping manner.
t (ten)	d (den)	The air comes from the lungs and is pushed out through the tongue being pressed against the ridge behind the teeth.
k (kill)	g (gill)	The air comes from the lungs and is pushed out between the back of the tongue and the roof of the mouth.
f (fan)	v (van)	The air comes from the lungs and is pushed out between the top row of teeth and the lower lip.
th (thin)	th (that)	The air comes from the lungs and is pushed out between the top row of teeth and the tongue.
s (sip)	z (zip)	The air comes from the lungs and is pushed through a narrow gap between the upper and lower sets of teeth. The air moves in a continuous stream. The lips are narrowed.
sh (ship)	3 (vision)	The air comes from the lungs and is pushed through a narrow gap between the upper and lower sets of teeth. The air moves in a continuous stream. The lips are pushed out and forward.
ch (chill)	j (Jill)	The air comes from the lungs and is quickly pushed through a narrow gap in the upper and lower sets of teeth. The air moves in a quick burst. The lips are pushed out and forward.

Figure 10.2 Consonant construction chart

Extension exercises

- Students choose from a range of vowel and consonant phonemes, and represent to each other/the class how each one is formed.
- Students test various consonants and determine whether they are voiced or voiceless.
- Students discover mouth shape and jaw position when articulating selected vowels.

Consonants can either be voiced or unvoiced, and sometimes go in pairs. Figure 10.2 is a guide as to how the major consonants of English are made. Example words containing these sounds are in brackets.

m (map)	The air comes from the lungs and is pushed out through the nose. The lips are pressed together.
n (nap)	The air comes from the lungs and is pushed out through the nose. The lips are open and the tongue is pressed against the ridge behind the upper set of teeth.
ng (si<u>ng</u>)	The air comes from the lungs and is pushed out through the nose. The lips are open and the tongue is pressed against the back of the roof of the mouth.
l (light)	The air comes from the lungs and is pushed past the tongue which lifts to meet the ridge behind the upper set of teeth.
r (right)	The air comes from the lungs and is pushed past the tongue which is raised and flexed towards the back of the mouth.
w (wit)	The air comes from the lungs and is pushed past the lips which form a tight circle.
h (hit)	The air comes from the lungs and is forced through a narrow channel far down the hollow tube, in a breathing manner.
wh (whip)	The air comes from the lungs and is pushed forcefully through rounded lips, rather like the sound made when blowing out a candle. Many accents of English have merged this sound with /w/.

Figure 10.3 Consonants not in pairs

Consonants not in pairs

The final five consonants in this chart (<l>, <r>, <w>, <h>, and 'wh') are considered by some to be tricky (Figure 10.3). This is because, by nature of their production, they function like consonants in that some turbulence is produced, but the obstruction in the tube is minimal in comparison with the other consonants.

Vowel construction

Vowels in the majority of accents of English fall into four broad categories: rounded, unrounded, open, and diphthongs (Figure 10.4).

For more information about vowels in other accents, see Appendix 1: Forgive me, Scotland.

Manner	Explanation	Sounds	Example Words
ROUNDED	The lips are not wide open and not pulled back, but pushed forward to varying degrees.	/o/ /aw/ /er/ /oo/ /uu/	got law her boot put
UNROUNDED	The lips are not wide open and not pushed forward but pulled back, to varying degrees.	/e/ /i/ /ee/	get sit tree
OPEN	The lips are wide open and not pulled back and not pushed forward.	/a/ /u/ /ar/	bat gum bar
DIPHTHONGS	The vowel sound begins rounded, unrounded or open but ends elsewhere.	/ay/ /ue/ /ie/ /oa/ /oy/ /ow/	day due die goat boy cow

Figure 10.4 Vowel construction chart

Example lesson

How many letters are in the alphabet? (26)

How many of those are vowels? (5, POSSIBLY 6)

What are they? (<A>, <E>, <I>, <O>, <U>, POSSIBLY <Y>)

So all the rest are consonants.

But have you ever wondered why these five letters, <a>, <e>, <i>, <o>, and <u>, are different to the others?

What we're going to do is a scientific experiment to work out the difference between vowels and consonants.

We are going to show the parts of the body that make speech sounds.

First, when I make a sound, what does it travel through to reach your ears? (AIR)

When you take air into your body, where does it go? (LUNGS)

So we need to start with a pair of lungs.

Did you know that the air travels from your lungs through a hollow tube in your throat and up into your mouth? In fact there are two hollow tubes there – one for food and water and the other for air. It's horrible when you get them mixed up isn't it?

Along this hollow tube, you have a set of muscles that vibrate and make sounds. Do you know what they're called? (VOCAL CORDS, LARYNX, VOICE BOX [Choose whichever is appropriate for your students])

Continuing up the hollow tube, the air from the lungs reaches the mouth. What things do you use in your mouth to make speech sounds? (TONGUE, TEETH, LIPS)

You can also demonstrate the importance of the tongue, teeth, and lips by asking the students to try and speak without using these various parts.

If you are confident that you can show how any consonant is made, let the students choose any consonant sound. If not, choose the sound you make for the letter <p>. This is the sound you make at the end of the word 'tap'. For more on consonant sounds and how they are made, please refer to the consonant construction chart (Figure 10.2).

Making a consonant sound

Take the magnetic letter <p> and place it on the lungs. As you demonstrate how the sound is made, move it through the hollow tube.

When you make the sound /p/, the air starts in your lungs, and comes up through the hollow tube. Does it pick up a sound at your voice box? (FOR /P/ THE ANSWER IS NO, FOR SOME CONSONANTS THE ANSWER WILL BE YES, see Figures 10.2 and 10.3)

The air reaches your mouth, and then what happens to it? (IT PRESSES AGAINST YOUR LIPS AND IS RELEASED IN A POPPING MANNER)

Take a magnetic letter <p> and move it from the lungs through to the mouth, showing what the tongue, teeth, and lips do to make that particular sound. With /p/, the air moves freely through the hollow tube until it hits the closed lips and has to force its way between them.

You can then ask some or all of the following questions:

Did the air come out freely, or did you have to make some effort to get it out? (EFFORT)

Did something get in the way? (YES, THE LIPS)

Was there something momentarily stopping that air from coming out? (YES, THE LIPS)

Did it have to push its way out? (YES)

Because you answered yes to the last three questions and said that some effort had to be made to get the sound out, we call this sound a consonant.

What you are trying to get the students to understand is that when making a consonant sound, there was some obstruction in the hollow tube. When they have answered some or all of the questions, tell them that that is the definition of a consonant.

You can repeat this with other consonants until the students are confident. It is often an advantage to contrast it with a vowel straight away. Take a magnetic letter <a> and move it from the lungs through to the mouth, showing that the air moves through unobstructed.

Now let's make a vowel sound. We'll make the sound /a/ as in 'at'.

The air starts in the lungs and moves along the hollow tube. Does it pick up a sound at the voice-box? (YES)

When it moves into your mouth, does anything get in the way or does it come out just like singing? (IT COMES OUT JUST LIKE SINGING)

This is a vowel.

11 What consonants say

With some basic concepts and tools in place, this and subsequent lessons now require a little more writing and use of worksheets. As Nichols (1985) says, 'Spelling is remembered best in your hand. It is the memory of your fingers moving the pencil to make a word that makes for accurate spelling'.

Consonants require less analysis than vowels. Most consonants in the alphabet have a 1:1 sound-to-symbol match, whereas vowel letters can represent at least two different sounds each.

We will deal with some basic consonant rules first. There are three separate lessons in this chapter:

1 The ⟨q⟩ rule
2 The ⟨c⟩ rule
3 The ⟨g⟩ rule

Lesson 1: The ⟨q⟩ rule

The letter ⟨q⟩ didn't exist in the English alphabet prior to the Norman invasion. 'Queen' was spelled 'cwen' and 'quick' was spelled 'cwic'. French scribes started inserting their 'qu' version in such words and then inconsiderately stopped pronouncing the /w/ sound, leaving English with words like 'unique' and 'quiche'. By then, many words containing /kw/ sounds in English had been standardised to be spelled 'qu', thus giving us the first consonant rule:

RULE: ⟨q⟩ is always written with the letter ⟨u⟩.

Students simply find three words which follow this rule. Students write these directly into their notebooks. Any exceptions can be examined using a word stories worksheet (Figure 3.3). There is a small list of ⟨q⟩-rule exceptions at the end of this chapter.

Lesson 2: The ⟨c⟩ rule

Draw attention to the letter ⟨c⟩ and discuss the sounds it can make.

RULE: when ⟨c⟩ comes before ⟨e⟩, ⟨i⟩, or ⟨y⟩, it MUST say /s/.

Students find three words which follow this rule. Students write these and any exceptions directly into their notebooks.

Lesson 3: The <g> rule

Draw attention to the letter <g> and discuss the sounds it can make.

RULE: when <g> comes before <e>, <i>, or <y>, it MAY say /j/.

NOTE: There are few exceptions to this rule, as <g> has the option of saying either of its two sounds before <e>, <i>, or <y>.

Pattern

The same three letters, <e>, <i>, and <y>, influence <c> and <g>.

For younger learners

In the Lindamood-Bell clinic where I first learned to teach this lesson, we used the image of a train to represent the <c> and <g> rules.

We called it the C-Train. It went chugging along the track from left to right, saying /k/k/k/k/ as it went. When it came to the signal containing the letters <e>, <i>, and <y>, it went down a different track, saying /s/s/s/s/ instead.

The same can be done with the G-Train. It went chugging along saying /g/g/g/g/ until it came to that same signal: <e>, <i>, and <y>. This time, though, instead of only having one track to go down, it had the choice of two: It could carry on saying /g/g/g/g/ but could also veer off and say /j/j/j/j/.

There is a video lesson on presenting the <c> and <g> rules on the Lifelong Literacy YouTube channel.

Summary

RULE: <q> is always written with the letter <u>.
RULE: when <c> comes before <e>, <i>, or <y>, it MUST say /s/.
RULE: when <g> comes before <e>, <i>, or <y>, it MAY say /j/.

Exceptions to the <q>, <c>, and <g> rules

The following is a list of words which break the <q> and <c> rules. They are rare words and in most cases are borrowed from other languages or have very specialised medical or scientific definitions. They are, however, acceptable for *Spelling for Life* in that they serve to demonstrate exceptions, an important tool for reinforcing rules. They also provide vocabulary enrichment and satisfy many a practitioner and student's curiosity regarding possible exceptions.

Because of their relative obscurity, definitions have been provided.

RULE: <q> is always written with <u>.

faqir A Muslim or Hindu monk

qanat A subterranean tunnel used for irrigation

qat Pronounced /cot/, a plant used for social chewing in parts of Africa and the Middle East

qawaali or **qawwali** Sufi devotional songs

qigong Chinese meditation system

qindar/qintar Unit of currency in Albania

qiviut Musk ox woollen undercoat

qoph The 19th letter of the Hebrew alphabet

qwerty The top row of letters on a modern keyboard

suq Variation of 'souk', a marketplace

tranqs Abbreviation for 'tranquillisers'

RULE: When <c> comes before <e>, <i>, or <y>, it MUST say /s/

caesarean Surgical delivery of offspring

caesura A break in the flow of sound usually in the middle of a line of verse

cephalic Of or relating to the head

coeliac Of or relating to the abdominal cavity

RULE: when <g> comes before <e>, <i>, or <y>, it MAY say /j/.

gaol Place of imprisonment, spelled this way in older literature, e.g. *The Ballad of Reading Gaol*

What consonants say spelling drill

1 Write out all the vowels in the alphabet.
2 Write out all the consonants.

SPELL:

1 queen
2 quick
3 quest
4 once
5 circle
6 cycle
7 get
8 give
9 buggy
10 age
11 gem
12 gym

12 Round the blend

Working 1:1 with primary school children allows me to monitor teaching trends in my local area. This micro-sample is often an indicator of general tendencies in teaching on a larger scale, and I try to confirm, as much as possible, the extent of what I've observed.

In the early years of this millennium, I started noticing my students incorporating the letter ‹y› into their lists of known vowels. I also saw a rise in simplistic but no less positive sayings like 'every word needs a vowel' and 'every sentence needs a verb'.

These are pleasing trends and give me much hope that linguistics is making some headway in teacher training. On the downside, however, there is quite a bit of false information and teaching trends which negatively impact students. Because I work with children who struggle as a result of these trends, I am especially aware of the damage they do. The children who come to me are like educational bellwethers, since they are the most affected by quality of teaching.

Recently I've been noticing an upswing in what I call *unwelcome intruders* and *missing persons*:

1. *Missing persons*: My students (most with some form of developmental language disorder) are increasingly prone to pronouncing a two-phoneme consonant cluster as one continuous sound, e.g. /b/ + /r/, as a rushed and indistinct /br/. When they come to spell ‹b› + ‹r› words, they say the two phonemes but represent them with the initial grapheme only. This results in words like *bring* spelled as ‹bing›.
2. *Unwelcome intruders*: When reading consonant-vowel-consonant (CVC) words, students insert consonants that aren't there – for instance, saying 'black' for *back* when reading.

I work with a population whose phonological awareness (PA) is typically low, so these two phenomena are relatively common, but I'm seeing it more frequently and in a wider group containing children whose PA scores are average or above.

I have a suspicion about the origins of this change. Of course, it's a theory at this stage, but I'd like to get to the bottom of it nonetheless. It concerns the teaching of 'blends', or more accurately, consonant clusters.

A consonant cluster can be defined as two or more adjacent consonants in a single syllable. In words, they can look like this:

C C V C
S T O P

or this:

C V C C
G I F T

or even this:

C C V C C
S T A M P

The phonemes in a simple syllable are relatively easy to segment, perceive, and represent. A CVC pattern, like 'bat' or 'mug', presents no significant difficulty in reading or spelling, especially if the phonemes can be represented with one letter. But as soon as a little bit of complexity is added, all hell breaks loose.

Take a CCVC pattern, e.g. 'stop', 'flat', or 'trip'. Greater effort and skill is required to perceive and represent that pattern.

One of the reasons for this is that speech sounds change a little bit when they appear in clusters. Their edges adapt to the sounds around them so that they can be said in a continuous stream. This is why clusters of consonants are sometimes referred to as *blends*, like blended coffee beans or blends of wine. The difference between consonants and coffee and wine, though, is that consonant blends can be pulled apart again.

This pulling apart, or segmenting, is as important as blending and yet seems to get short shrift. By the way, *shrift* is an example of a relatively uncommon CCVCC pattern.

Teaching blending in the absence of segmenting is like teaching addition without subtraction. And yet I see it all the time.

There are now many commercial 'phonics' resources that contain slideshows and worksheets that depict consonant clusters in isolation (e.g. bl-, cl-, dr-). Classes of children are instructed to recite each one rapidly as one continuous sound.

Now, many children will learn to read and spell regardless of the quality of the method used to teach them. This is all very well. But many won't. Many rely on expert, explicit, systematic teaching of the structure of words to help establish a foundation for fluency, vocabulary, and comprehension. Teaching blends as one sound is not this.

So how do we tackle this problem? Teacher knowledge is the key. 'Blend' training is done with the best intentions, but there is no research evidence that teaching a cluster as one sound is good for students, and studies have shown no additional increase in word-reading speed when poor readers are taught blends (Marinus et al. 2012).

Firstly, let's untangle some definitions commonly used interchangeably:

- **blend** (verb) – the process of pronouncing phonemes rapidly to form a spoken word
- **cluster** (noun) – a group of adjacent phonemes in speech or a group of adjacent graphemes in writing

- **diphthong** - a vowel sound in speech made using two places of articulation but requiring only one impulse of the voice, e.g. /oy/, which begins with round lips and ends with lips stretched back and can be said in one impulse
- **digraph** - a written symbol which uses two letters but represents one sound, e.g. <sh>, <ch>, <ph>

Secondly, let's make sure we're giving children plenty of practice in segmenting the sounds in words as well as blending them. Presenting ready-made 'blends' and 'blend' worksheets is folly. By all means, teach children *to* blend, but as part of a word or a morpheme, not by itself.

A consonant cluster is a lifeless zombie occupying the no man's land between phoneme and morpheme. Teaching these meaningless units only adds several hundred more pieces of code to be learned for no semantic purpose.

One exception to this is the cluster tw-. This denotes the number two in a range of English words: 'two', 'twice', 'twin', 'twelve', 'twenty', 'twist', 'twine', 'between', 'twilight', and the Twix chocolate bar (it has two fingers).

English spelling is an elegant, pattern-based system of writing, which becomes apparent if examined thoughtfully. Spelling only appears to be random and arbitrary if its patterns are introduced randomly and arbitrarily.

It is possible for consonant clusters to be introduced systematically. There is scope for a great deal of valuable linguistic analysis on this subject. Using ready-made 'blend' sheets reduces the opportunity to develop this linguistic knowledge.

In other words, my question is, in ready-made 'blend' exercises, whose brain does the analysis, the compiler or the student?

Presenting already-formed consonant clusters is a sure way of robbing students of the chance to form and test hypotheses regarding the constraints of the writing system. It takes the scientific process and therefore the beauty and wonder out of the task of learning to spell.

This lesson gives students the chance to generate their own clusters and apply that knowledge to their writing.

By creating, storing, retrieving, and problem-solving with this information, students are working in a way that is far more likely to enhance orthographic mapping than filling out haphazard 'blend' sheets.

> English spelling is an elegant, pattern-based system of writing, which becomes apparent if examined thoughtfully.

Lesson plan

Materials

Two 4" × 6" index cards for each student, or any sturdy, lined card. Size can vary according to student age.

Duration

1-2 hours per card.

Step 1

Distribute a Consonant Start Card and write all the consonants in the alphabet on the top line and the digraphs underneath.

Digraphs have two letters but one sound. The common digraphs below the first line are all written with the letter <h>. You can ask your students to figure out what they are. So far, their cards should look like this:

Consonant Starts
b c d f g h j k l m n p qu r s t v w x y z
ch, ph, sh, th, wh

NOTE: Digraphs here are not to be confused with two-letter sequences where one letter is silent, like the <mb> in 'dumb'. Silent-letter words belong in families as listed in Chapter 27: More fascinating patterns.

Rather, with the exception of <ph>, which entered our language via the Roman and Greek alphabets, the digraphs <ch>, <th>, <sh>, and <wh> are an Anglo-Saxon solution to a Roman problem. When adopting the Roman alphabet, Anglo-Saxon scribes had to invent symbols for the sounds /ch/, /th/, /sh/, and /wh/.

The digraph <wh> occurs only in some accents of English now and has, in many cases, reverted to a /w/ sound, rendering words like 'weather' and 'whether' homophones.

Step 2

Systematically generate all the legal word-initial consonant clusters in English. Begin, if you have to, by taking the first consonant, the letter <b>, and combining it with the letter <c>. Ask if this combination can begin words. You may have to keep doing this all the way through to the first legal cluster, <bl>, and again until the next one, <br>.

Moving on to the letter <c>, a pattern starts to emerge, i.e. <cl> and <cr> are legal word-initially. The letter <d> also blends with <r>, and the letter <f> blends with <l> and <r>, and so on.

This might be a quick process, this might be slow, depending on what your students already know. What is important here is that students start to notice the patterns, i.e. that there is a small, limited set of word-initial consonants that blends with an even smaller, limited set of second consonants (<l>, <r>, <w> for all consonants, excepting a slightly bigger set with the letter <s>).

Why do you think this is? What do you notice about those second consonants?[1]

On the next line, figure out the following clusters:

bl, br, cl, cr, dr, dw, fl, fr, gl, gr, pl, pr

and on the next line these clusters:

sc, sk, sl, sm, sn, sp, st, sw, tr, tw

---

[1]   The consonants <l>, <r>, and <w> can also be classified as *semi-vowels* or *glides*, due to the nature of their articulation. They are 'frictionless', that is, they can be articulated continuously and so lend themselves to blending with other consonants in the second position.

and the uncommon clusters

    chr, phl, phr, thw

There are, arguably, other possible ones, such as ‹cz› and ‹ts›. They aren't included here, as they appear in a tiny family of words, usually borrowed from other languages where such clusters are common ('czar', 'tsunami').

    The cards now look like this:

Consonant Starts

    b c d f g h j k l m n p qu r s t v w x y z
    ch, ph, th, sh, wh
    bl, br, cl, cr, dr, dw, fl, fr, gl, gr, kr, pl, pr
    sc, sk, sl, sm, sn, sp, st, sw, tr, tw
    chr, phl, phr, thw

NOTE on the letter ‹y›: Word-initially, the letter ‹y› can be classed as a consonant, but the moment it appears word-internally or word-finally it usually represents a vowel. Therefore, when trying to generate clusters, skip ‹y› as a second letter.

    See Chapter 12 for a whole lesson on ‹y›.

Step 3

There is a consonant card for endings too. It differs slightly from the Consonant Start Card because different rules apply to word-endings. This brings us into the intriguing world of Illegal Letters and their solutions (Chapter 13).

    Turn to the Consonant End Card and write the single consonants on the first line. To show that they are word-final, add a dash before each consonant. Be sure to point out that ‹j›, ‹q›, and ‹v› do not appear word-finally in English words, and that ‹y› is only a consonant at the start of a word.

    ‹Q› can appear word-finally, but only in the presence of the letters ‹u› and ‹e›.

    The top row will look like this:

Consonant Ends

    -b -c -d -f -g -k -l -m -n -p -que -r -s -t -x -z

Step 4

Now look for consonants that can double up at the ends of words and write them on line 2. These are referred to in my practice as 'The Doublers' and *commonly* appear together at the ends of words. They are ‹ff›, ‹ll›, and ‹ss›.

    I have not included uncommon doublers, such as ‹bb› ('ebb'), ‹dd› ('add', 'odd'), ‹gg› ('egg'), ‹nn› ('inn'), ‹rr› ('err', 'burr', 'purr'), ‹tt› ('matt', 'watt', 'butt', 'putt', 'batt'), ‹zz› ('jazz', 'buzz', 'whizz', 'fizz', 'fuzz'). They are better learned in word families with the feature 'uncommon doubler'.

Now the card looks like this:

Consonant Ends
-b -c -d -f -g -k -l -m -n -p -que -r -s -t -x -z
-ff -ll -ss

Step 5

Systematically generate the third line using <h> and including the 'ck' and 'ng' digraphs.

Consonant Ends
b -c -d -f -g -k -l -m -n -p -que -r -s -t -x -z
-ff -ll -ss
-ch -sh -th -ph -ck -ng

NOTE: The letter <h> appears word-finally in two main ways:

* as part of a consonant digraph (<ch>, <th>, <sh>);
* as part of a vowel digraph to generate a very small set of interjections (<ah>, <eh>, <oh>, <uh>)

It does not make a /h/ sound word-finally.
    Similarly, the letter <w> does not appear word-finally unless it is part of a vowel digraph (<aw>, <ew>, <ow>).

Step 6

Now generate the fourth and fifth lines. As you can see, the pattern of word-final clusters is really quite limited.

Consonant Ends
-b -c -d -f -g -k -l -m -n -p -que -r -s -t -x -z
-ff, -ll, -ss
-ch -sh -th -ph -ck -ng
-ct -lf -lk -lm -lp -lt -mp -nd -nk -lt -nt -pt
-sc -sk -sp -st

NOTE about the letter <s>: You can also add the letter <s> to many of these endings to form a plural noun ('lamps') or a third person singular verb ('costs'). I have not included this because it is a suffix, and follows a different set of rules. By all means, have your students note the flexibility of the letter <s> and get them to work out for themselves the reason for its prevalence.

Other clusters

There are other legal, uncommon consonant clusters (e.g. <mt> in 'dreamt'), including three-letter ones (<str> in 'string', <spr> as in 'spring', <scr> as in 'scratch', etc.). For simplicity at this stage, only two-letter clusters have been included here, but by all means, teach the three-consonant clusters at your discretion.

I have also not included graphemes such as <dge> ('edge') or <tch> ('witch'). Examples of these are grouped in families and generated using the Consonant Starts plus a vowel. Fascinating patterns emerge when generating these families.

Once the cards have been filled in, they provide a stable framework for understanding and generating reliable spellings for a great many other words.

13 Illegal Letters

The Illegal Letters are the five letters that are not permitted to be at the end of a word in English. They are <i>, <j>, <q>, <u>, and <v>. There are historical reasons for the Illegal Letter rule, usually to do with typographical or phonetic clarity.

That is not to say that words don't end with the sounds commonly associated with those letters ('fly', 'badge', 'unique', 'glue', 'have'). It's just that our rules don't allow <i>, <j>, <q>, <u>, or <v> to represent those sounds in that position.

Knowing the Illegal Letters and their solutions gives learners reliable strategies for tackling the ends of words.

The letter <e> provides a solution in all cases. Let the students figure this out by asking them to detect a common pattern once the worksheet is done.

Lesson plan

Skill level

- Middle primary: dictionary use and higher-order vocabulary is necessary here. This is not to stop any discussion of Illegal Letters with younger learners, but the worksheets can only be fully done by older learners.

Materials

- Illegal Letters worksheet (Figure 10.2)
- Dictionary
- Word stories worksheet (Figure 1.4)

Duration

20 minutes per letter.

Step 1

Brainstorm the five Illegal Letters and write them alphabetically on the worksheet.

Step 2

Review each Illegal Letter and work out possible solutions for each one, e.g. for the letter <i>, the /ie/ sound at the end of a word is spelled with a <y> or <ie>.

Letter	Solution	Examples	Exceptions	Story
i	-y, -ie	my pie	ski alibi I hi fungi	Norwegian Latin/legal old slang scientific
j	-ge, -dge	cage badge	haj raj	Arabic Indian
q	-que	pique unique	qwerty suq	acronym Arabic
u	-ue	glue true	flu menu you	abbreviation French old
v	-ve	love give weave	spiv rev	slang abbreviation

Figure 13.1 Illegal Letters example worksheet

Step 3

Find exceptions for each Illegal Letter (if possible) and write them in the 'exceptions' column. In the column adjacent to that, write each word story, i.e. why the word is exceptional by referring to a dictionary. If students have begun a word stories worksheet (Figure 3.4), they can add words to this during the lesson.

RULE: You may not use the letters <i>, <j>, <q>, <u>, or <v> at the end of English words. They are illegal.

ALTERNATIVE CATCHY RULE: <i>, <j>, <q>, <u>, <v> … at the end of a word they cannot be!

Illegal Letters spelling drill

1 untie
2 badge
3 unique
4 true
5 weave
6 carry
7 fridge
8 glue
9 above
10 crazy
11 arrange
12 plaque

Letter	Solution	Examples	Exceptions	Story
i				
j				
q				
u				
v				

Figure 13.2 Illegal Letters blank worksheet

14 The single vowels

Without vowels, it would be very hard to communicate. Every word, and every syllable within a word, must have a vowel or vowel-like sound, otherwise we would not be able to say or hear words clearly at all.

Syllabic consonants

If you're thinking of possible exceptions to this, such as the second syllable in words like 'double', 'chasm', or 'button', then you have come across what is sometimes termed a 'syllabic consonant'.

The /l/ sound in 'double', the /m/ sound in 'chasm', and the /n/ in 'button' are all sonorant enough to form a syllable.

Wells (2008) states that although phonetic transcription of these syllables can occur without using a vowel symbol, they are often represented by schwa, /ə/, plus a consonant, thus proving that at the phonetic level at least, a vowel sound is still present in every syllable (see Chapter 23: Schwa).

> Every word, and every syllable within a word, must have a vowel sound, otherwise we would not be able to say or hear words clearly at all.

The scope of this chapter

We will deal here with single vowels, not vowel combinations. Two-letter vowels will be dealt with in Chapter 21: The Vowel Generator.

An important by-product of this lesson is the reinforcement of the concept of letter *sounds* being separate from letter *names*. This is an important principle. It is surprising how many students there are who do not know the difference and who become better spellers and readers after understanding this distinction (Wolf 2001). Appendix 3: The Triangle Game presents an additional lesson on helping learners differentiate between the two.

A note about vowel sounds

Every vowel letter can be associated with at least two sounds:

1   The first and most commonly associated sounds for the vowels are in 'b<u>a</u>t', 'g<u>e</u>t', 's<u>i</u>t', 'n<u>o</u>t', 'g<u>u</u>m' for <a>, <e>, <i>, <o>, <u>. These are sometimes known as the 'short sound'.

2   The second common sounds are the letter names, e.g. 'b<u>a</u>con', 'm<u>e</u>', 't<u>i</u>ger', '<u>o</u>pen', '<u>u</u>nit' for <a>, <e>, <i>, <o>, <u> again. These are sometimes known as the 'long sound'.

In the case of <a>, <o>, and <u>, additional sounds are associated with these letters. These are mentioned in the lesson.

Why we don't use 'short sound/long sound'

In my practice, we do not use the terms 'short sound' and 'long sound'. Here's why:

One of the crucial building blocks for literacy is phonemic awareness. This is the ability to perceive the number, order, sameness, and difference of sounds within words. Low phonemic awareness is often a contributing factor to difficulty with spelling.

If perception of sounds within words is a problem, then categorising sounds based on minute, temporal signals effectively bars anyone with low phonemic awareness from self-checking and correcting.

Put another way, a student who struggles to perceive the difference between the words 'bit' and 'beet', or who cannot perceive that there is a missing phoneme in the word 'sand' when the target word is 'stand', is highly unlikely to reliably perceive how long it takes to say a vowel.

Far better to use terms already familiar, i.e. 'sound' and 'name'.

A vowel's *sound* refers to the common phonemic association for symbols that children are taught from nursery onwards.

A vowel's *name* is also taught virtually from birth through alphabet names and songs.

These are familiar terms that require no extra processing.

Why do some vowels say their names?

Vowels don't say their name for no reason, a fact worth stressing right from the beginning. When a single vowel (<a>, <e>, <i>, <o>, or <u>) says its name, there are two main reasons:

1   It is at the end of a syllable.

2   It is being made to say its name by an adjacent <e>. Word-finally, if it is separated from the <e> by a consonant, this is also known as a 'split digraph', e.g. 'cane', 'Pete', 'hope', 'pine', and 'cute'.

A note on split digraphs

There are numerous ways to observe and explain spelling. Some terms go in and out of fashion. For instance, it was once popular to call frequently misspelled words 'demons'. It is less fashionable to attach such negative connotations to words these days, even though it might be tempting.

Some terms describe the same rules. For instance, 'Magic E' and 'Bossy E' are equally valid and concern the same rule.

There is a common term nowadays to describe what is happening when a word-final <e> is acting to signal that a preceding vowel is saying its name, even though the two letters are separated by one consonant. This term is 'split digraph'.

'Cane', 'Pete', 'pine', 'hope', and 'cute' can all be described as split digraph words.

I do not use this term in my practice. Here's why: First, the term 'digraph' is misleading. It implies that <ae>, <ee>, <ie>, <oe>, and <ue> are common two-letter combinations, whereas any cryptographical research will show that there are many much more common vowel digraphs in English (<er> and <or> being two exceedingly common ones).

In fact, <ae> is rare, only really occurring in words to do with air ('aeronaut', 'aerosol'), Greek words ('anaemia', 'archaeology'), and Latin plurals ('algae', 'antennae').

Second, this term doesn't account for all the other vowel digraphs in English (see Chapter 21: The Vowel Generator), such as <ai>, <oa>, <ew> etc.

My preference, and one that has wider application, is to attribute the vowel name phenomenon in 'cane' etc. to the first job of Final Silent E.

Final Silent E Job 1: makes a vowel say its name even if it has to jump over a consonant to do it (Chapter 16).

I personally find it easier and more logical to look into the various jobs of Final Silent E. Talking about an isolated set of digraphs of varying commonality that, for some unknown reason, just happen to have suddenly been split apart by a random consonant simply doesn't make sense to me.

Teaching that words like 'cane' etc., have an evolution of pronunciation and spelling can only be beneficial. Take the example word 'cake', which was originally a two-syllable word with the final <e> making a sound, a little like a schwa or /uh/. The final vowel became less distinct over time until it disappeared altogether, but the letter that stood for it remained (see Glossary: Standardisation). The silent letter still exists as a signal that the preceding vowel says its name.

The term 'split digraph' takes focus from the actual principles which operate the spelling of these words.

Lesson plan

Skill level

- Handwriting
- Phonemic awareness
- Chapter 10: The difference between vowels and consonants

Materials

- Figure 14.1 Single vowels worksheet
- Refer to the sound-to-symbol notation section at the beginning of this book if necessary

Duration

10–15 minutes per vowel.

	Sound	Name	Extra sounds		
a					
e					
i					
o					
u					

RULE:

Figure 14.1 Single vowels blank worksheet

	Sound	Name	Extra sounds		
a	bat	bacon	bat	ball	swan
e	get	me			
i	sit	tiger			
o	not	open	do	mother	
u	gum	unit	blue	put	

> **RULE:** When a vowel is at the end of a syllable it says its name.

Figure 14.2 Single vowels example worksheet

Step 1

Discuss the importance of vowels by having students write their names, cross out the vowels, and then try to shout their vowel-free names.

Step 2

Distribute the single vowels worksheet. Tell students that the most common sound that <a> makes is /a/ as in 'bat'. Write 'bat' in the 'sound' column next to the letter <a>.

Step 3

Ask for the name of the letter, and write the example word, 'bacon', in the second column. Tell students why <a> says its name at the end of the syllable and write the rule:

RULE: When a vowel is at the end of a syllable it says its name.

Step 4

Tell students the other sounds <a> can make and write example words in the 'extra sounds' boxes. The sounds are /ah/ as in 'bath', /aw/ as in 'ball' and /o/ as in 'swan'. These extra sounds are based on a standard English accent.

NOTE: I have not included rules for these extra sounds, though their existence is rule-based. For instance, the letter <a> often says /ar/ ('bath', 'father', 'lava') when followed by <th> or <v>.

The reason for this is that, though interesting, it is sometimes necessary to draw the line as to how many rules are presented. I have used my judgement in this case and prefer to include examples rather than more rules, as their application is usually limited to a small set of words.

If my students do spot the patterns in these words, all the better. There is no reason not to discuss them if they come up, but formally teaching them at this level can be distracting.

Step 5

Repeat the process for the rest of the vowels.

Example lesson

> Now that you know what vowels and consonants are, I want you to tell me why we need vowels. Why can't we have a language with consonants only?
>
> To answer this fully, I'm going to take a name, such as Sam, and take away the vowel. What would that name be now? (SM)
>
> Let's write 'Sam' down, but because we live in a world without vowels, we'll cross out the <a>.
>
> What if this 'Sm' person were walking across the street ... listening to some loud music through his headphones ... and not looking where he was going ... and there was a truck coming ... and you tried to call out to him to watch out ... but his name is 'Sm', so all you could do is shout ... 'SM!!!' What would happen? ('SM' WOULD GET HIT BY THE TRUCK!)

> Shout 'Sm!' as loud as you can. Without the vowel, it will sound muffled and short, as if someone is holding their hand over your mouth.
>
> You can also repeat this using your name or your students' names. In a group setting, get students to come up to the board and cross out the vowels in their name and have the other students try to shout the new word.
>
> My favourite student for this exercise was a boy called Hamish. His name became 'Hmsh!' – the sort of name you would give a pet dinosaur. He loved that.

> Why can't we shout people's names when there are no vowels? (BECAUSE VOWELS CARRY THE MOST SOUND IN WORDS BECAUSE THEY ARE UNOBSTRUCTED. YOU CANNOT SHOUT A CONSONANT.)
>
> For vowels, the hollow tube that carries your speech sounds is open, letting the air carry the sound without anything getting in the way.
>
> So that's why we need vowels. We need vowels in every word, and not only in every word, but also in every syllable in every word.

If students do not understand what a syllable is, please refer to Chapter 7 and teach them this concept now.

If students have some understanding of what a syllable is, you are ready to move on. Distribute the single vowels worksheet.

What is the first vowel in the alphabet? (A)

Write it in the first square on the first line. We are going to show all the sounds that the letter <a> can make by writing some example words.

The first and most common sound that <a> makes is /a/. And the example word we are going to write is 'bat'. Write it in the second square.

The next sound that <a> makes is its name, /ay/. The example word is 'bacon'. Write it next to 'bat'.

We are going to look at why the <a> says its name, /ay/, in the word 'bacon'.

The first syllable in 'bacon' is 'ba-'.

NOTE: We split the word at this point because, when breaking words in English, our minds automatically tend to start syllables with consonants. Syllable breaking is rule-based, and all mature readers and spellers have internalised these rules whether they're conscious of them or not.

Is the vowel at the beginning or at the end of the syllable? (AT THE END)

So the rule here is that <a> will say its name, /ay/, at the end of a syllable. Vowels never say their name for no reason. There is always something making a single vowel say its name. In this word, it's as if the letter <a> is on the edge of a cliff, and without a consonant to support it, it falls off the cliff and shouts its name, 'aaaaaaaaaaay', as it falls. Draw an arrow underneath the letter <a> to show it falling off the cliff.

Now write down the rule.

RULE: When a vowel is at the end of a syllable it says its name.

NOTE: This section is for a standard English accent and its close relatives only. Scottish, Irish, Cornish, Canadian, and General American accents are amongst those that do not distinguish vowels in these words from the first sound that <a> makes. If this is not relevant for your accent, please skip the next two sounds of the letter <a> and go to the last sound.

If this makes you feel left out, please see Appendix 1: Forgive me, Scotland.

The next sound that <a> makes is /ah/. The example word is 'bath'. Write it next to 'bacon'.

    The next sound that <a> makes is /aw/. The example word is 'ball'. Write it next to 'bath'.

NOTE: All accents of English can use this part of the lesson again.

The next sound that <a> makes is /o/. The example word is 'swan'. Write it next to 'ball'.

    Repeat this process for the rest of the vowels, making sure you note the sound/name distinction.

The single vowels spelling drill

1 bath
2 get
3 sit
4 paper
5 swim
6 mother
7 yet
8 give
9 unit
10 bat
11 tiger
12 swan
13 ball
14 path
15 met
16 bacon
17 swap
18 to
19 thump
20 felt

15   The letter ⟨y⟩

After examining the various single vowels, it's time to deal with the letter ⟨y⟩. Experience has taught me, though, that linking ⟨y⟩ to the letters ⟨e⟩ and ⟨i⟩ is more relevant, memorable, and applicable than leaving ⟨y⟩ to be dealt with in isolation. This is why I often insert this lesson after teaching ⟨e⟩ and ⟨i⟩ and before the rest of the vowels in the preceding chapter.

The letter ⟨y⟩ can represent both vowels and consonants, depending on its position in the word.

For instance, in the word 'lazy', ⟨y⟩ is clearly making an unobstructed vowel sound, something like /ee/ or /i/, depending on your accent. What is clear is that word-final ⟨y⟩ is articulated as a vowel.

When an /ie/ sound is required at the end of a word (e.g. 'fly', 'sky', and 'comply'), the letter ⟨i⟩ is not permitted because it is one of the five Illegal Letters (Chapter 13). The letter ⟨y⟩ resolves this by taking on the /ie/ sound and because it is permitted word-finally.

In the word 'gym', ⟨y⟩ again is making an /i/ sound. This is often the case in Greek-derived words. Therefore, word-internal ⟨y⟩ is also commonly pronounced as a vowel.

Word-initial ⟨y⟩, such as in 'yacht' and 'yes', can arguably be classified as a vowel or a consonant sound. Slowed down, the ⟨y⟩ in yacht sounds like a combination of the vowel sounds /ee/ and /uh/. But you wouldn't say 'an yacht' or 'an yellow ribbon', so from a phonological perspective, your brain classifies word-initial ⟨y⟩ as a consonant.

The concept of word-initial and word-internal ⟨y⟩ being a vowel also ties in with and expands students' knowledge of the five Illegal Letters and their solutions.

> The letter ⟨y⟩ can represent both vowels and consonants, depending on its position in the word.

Lesson plan

Materials

Figure 15.2 The letter ⟨y⟩ worksheet.

Duration

30–60 minutes.

Step 1

Distribute the worksheet and introduce the concept of 'stunt doubles' in movies, and how their jobs are similar to those of the letter ‹y›, i.e. they go where others cannot (see example dialogue below).

Step 2

Write 'laze' on the board and work out why that is the wrong spelling for 'lazy'. Find more examples of ‹y› substituting for an /ee/ sound in the place that ‹e› cannot make a sound (i.e. word-finally). Students write 'lazy' in column 1.

Step 3

Write 'fli' on the board and ask why you don't spell 'fly' this way. Ask for a solution, which is to use ‹y›. Find other examples of ‹y› substituting for an /ie/ sound where the letter ‹i› cannot go (i.e. word-finally again).

Step 4

Write 'gym' in column 3 and explain Greek-derived words. Finding examples will be trickier, since words that we borrowed from Greek are typically (there's one) literary and scientific terms. Younger students don't have to completely fill in the whole column.

Example lesson

Before we look at the next vowel in the alphabet, I want you to think about the film industry – in particular, the actors that play the big parts in the big films.

Now most of these people are very good-looking and their famous faces and bodies are worth millions of dollars. The problem is, in many of their films they have to do dangerous things like leaping out of planes and being blown up and so forth. How do these beautiful people still manage to do all this dangerous stuff without being in danger? (THEY USE STUNT DOUBLES)

These people sometimes can't be in a scene because it's too dangerous, so they have specially trained stunt doubles to stand in for them. The same thing happens with the vowels ‹e› and ‹i›. There are certain places in words that ‹e› and ‹i› cannot be. So we have to use the stunt-letter ‹y›. It actually makes three vowel sounds and takes the place of ‹e› and ‹i› at the end of words and sometimes stands in for ‹i› inside words too.

The first vowel sound that ‹y› makes is /ee/. The example word that we are going to use for its first sound is 'lazy'.

Write 'laze' on the board and ask why 'lazy' can't be written this way.

Most students say, 'Because it doesn't look right', which is true enough. A more accurate answer is that the letter ‹e› is silent at the end of words. More on this in Chapter 16: Final Silent E.

Why?	1. When ‹e› cannot be there	2. When ‹i› cannot be there	3. Greek ‹i›
	lazy	fly	gym
	baby	why	analyse
	angry	by	hyphen
	every	try	synonym
	fifty	spy	type

RULE: When you cannot use the letter ‹e› or ‹i›, use ‹y›.

Figure 15.1 Letter ‹y› example worksheet

The letter ‹e› is silent at the end of words so it can't be there. But we need something to make the /ee/ sound at the end of 'lazy'. What is the solution to this problem? (WRITE ‹Y› INSTEAD OF ‹E›)

Yes, use the stunt-letter ‹y›, not the letter ‹e›, nor the letters ‹ey›, ‹ie›, or ‹ee›. There are only a few words in English that end in ‹ey› compared to thousands that end in ‹y›. A great thing to remember is that if you can get away with using one letter instead of two, then use one. This is the first lesson in keeping it simple.

This is an opportunity to erase the common, erroneous placing of ‹ey› at the end of unfamiliar words (e.g. 'ladey', 'angrey', 'happey').

Doing this is a common coping strategy. There are only two words in the Fry 1000 List ('money' and 'valley') that end in ‹ey›, so drill into your students' minds that ‹y› is a much more common ending when an /ee/ sound is needed word-finally.

You may also want to study an ‹ey› word family based on this feature. This is a list of words that do end in these two letters. This family will be smaller and easier to learn than the family of words containing only ‹y› at the end. There is an alphabetical list of common ‹ey› words in Chapter 4: Word families.

Why?	1. When <e> cannot be there	2. When <i> cannot be there	3. Greek <i>

RULE:

Figure 15.2 Letter ‹y› blank worksheet

Write 'lazy' in the next box.

The next sound that ‹y› makes is /ie/. The example word is 'fly'. Write it next to 'lazy'.

Do you know why we use the letter ‹y› in this word? Why can't we write it ‹f-l-i›?

The reason we can't do this is because ‹i› is an Illegal Letter. That means that you cannot use it at the end of a word in English.

Another sound that ‹y› makes is /i/. The letter ‹y› also replaces the letter ‹i› in words that we borrowed from Greek. So if it's a Greek root and an /i/ sound, chances are you need a ‹y› there. Our example word is 'gym'. Write it next to 'fly'.

It's now time to write the ‹y› rule.

RULE: When you cannot use the letter ‹e› or ‹i›, use ‹y›.

The letter ‹y› spelling drill

1 gym
2 lady
3 cry
4 type
5 angry
6 party
7 try
8 twenty
9 very
10 fly

16 Final Silent E, Jobs 1-3

In this lesson you will teach students how to use the letter <e> at the end of words.

When <e> comes at the end of a word, it is not heard. It is silent. We used to pronounce <e> at the ends of words in some cases. In other cases it was simply used as a marker, either to cancel plurals or to change pronunciation of preceding graphemes. This lesson is about these signals. They are called the Jobs of Final Silent E.

There are many names for the letter E at the end of words. Some call it 'Bossy E', others call it 'Magic E', and so on. Our complete name for it is Final Silent E.

The jobs are as follows:

1 Final Silent E makes a vowel say its name, even if it has to jump over a consonant to do it ('cane', 'hope', 'pine').
2 Final Silent E makes <c> say /s/ and <g> say /j/ ('dance', 'rage').
3 Final Silent E stops words from ending with Illegal Letters ('have', 'due').

Job 4 is slightly more complex and requires deeper analysis. It has a separate lesson plan and example lesson. It goes like this:

4 Final Silent E can give the last syllable a vowel ('able', 'rifle', 'muzzle').

In some instances, Final Silent E is simply reflecting a pronunciation that is no longer used and/ or is not signalling anything except the word's origins. This can be explained as No Job E. The tricky part is recalling the spelling. At Lifelong Literacy, we mark all instances of Final Silent E with a small cross underneath and we say the letter <e> for spelling when revising the word.

Some examples:

are, done, come, some, giraffe, cigarette

A list of high-frequency Final Silent E words can be found at the end of this chapter.
The benefits of this lesson are:

- Students learn not to randomly place <e> at the end of words. This is a common coping strategy.
- Students get a deeper understanding of the correct function of the letter <e>.
- Students don't mistakenly pronounce the <e> at the end of words when sounding them out. This makes them better readers.

- Students learn another important lesson on how a vowel can say its name. This makes it easier to spell and read words using the correct letters and sounds.

Lesson plan

Skill level

- Handwriting
- Sound-symbol skills
- The difference between a letter sound ('short sound') and a letter name ('long sound')
- Chapter 13: Illegal Letters

Materials

- Figures 16.1-16.4 Final Silent E 1-3 worksheet
- Figure 16.5 Final Silent E wordlist

Error pattern

'If in doubt, put an <e> at the end.'

Duration

30-45 minutes for the entirety of Jobs 1-3, including No Job E.

Final Silent E Job 1

Step 1

Distribute Final Silent E worksheet.

Step 2

Add Final Silent E to the words and compare the vowel sound from old to new.

Step 3

Write Job 1: Final Silent E makes a vowel say its name, even if it has to jump over a consonant to do it.

Step 4

Find other examples and write them in the spaces provided.

Final Silent E Job 2

Step 1

Go to 'dance' and 'large' in the next two squares.

Step 2

Students attempt to pronounce the words omitting Final Silent E.

Step 3

Write Job 2: Final Silent E makes <c> say /s/ and <g> say /j/.

Step 4

Find other examples and write them in the spaces provided.

Final Silent E special note

Step 1

Students attempt to pronounce the words 'race' and 'rage' omitting Final Silent E.

Step 2

Write:

NOTE: Final Silent E can do two jobs at the same time.

Step 3

Find other examples and write them in the spaces provided.

Final Silent E Job 3

Step 1

Work out why 'due' and 'give' don't look right when omitting <e>.

Step 2

Write Job 3: Final Silent E stops words from ending with Illegal Letters.

Step 3

Find other examples and write them in the spaces provided.

		New word	Examples
can	+e =		
pet	+e =		
pin	+e =		
hop	+e =		
cut	+e =		

Add Final Silent E.

Final Silent E Job 1

_____

_____

_____

Figure 16.1 Final Silent E Job 1

		New word	Examples
dance	-e =		
large	-e =		
race	-e =		
rage	-e =		

Take away Final Silent E.

Final Silent E Job 2

_____

_____

_____

Note:

_____

_____

_____

Figure 16.2 Final Silent E Job 2

		New word	Examples
due	-e =		
give	-e =		

Take away Final Silent E.

Final Silent E Job 3

_____

_____

_____

Figure 16.3 Final Silent E Job 3

		New word	Examples
are	-e =		
come	-e =		

Sometimes, Final Silent E . . .

_____

_____

_____

Figure 16.4 Final Silent E no job

Example lessons

Final Silent E Job 1

What is the most common letter in the English language? (THE LETTER ⟨E⟩)

Did you know that the letter ⟨e⟩ is very powerful? You may have heard it called 'Magic E' or 'Bossy E' before, because of all the things it does. Now we are going to look at ⟨e⟩ at the ends of words and all the things it can do there.

On your worksheet, there are five words in the first column. Let's see what sound the vowels are making in those words.

Now let's add Final Silent E. What word? (CANE)

Which vowel is making a sound? (⟨A⟩)

What sound? (/AY/)

Is that its first sound or its name? (NAME)

If I take away the ⟨e⟩ at the end of 'cane', what does it say now? ('CAN')

What sound does the vowel make? (/A/ AS IN 'CAT')

Is that its sound or its name? (SOUND)

So what does the ⟨e⟩ do to that word? (IT MAKES THE ⟨A⟩ SAY ITS NAME)

Where did the ⟨e⟩ come in this word? (AT THE END)

That is why we call it Final E.

Did ⟨e⟩ make a sound of its own in this word? (NO)

That is why we call it Final Silent E.

In 'cane', Final Silent E is doing its first job. Let's write it down:

> JOB 1: Final Silent E makes a vowel say its name, even if it has to jump over a consonant to do it.

We are now going to add Final Silent E to each of these words. Let's see what happens when we do.

Final Silent E Job 2

Let's take the word 'dance'. What would this word sound like if you took the Final Silent E away? ('DANC')

But the word we want is 'dance'.

So can you tell me what the Final Silent E is doing in the word dance? (FINAL SILENT E IS MAKING THE ⟨C⟩ SAY /S/)

This is the first part of the next job. Write it down.

> JOB 2: Final Silent E makes ⟨c⟩ say /s/

Now let's look at the word 'large'. What would this word sound like if you took the Final Silent E away? ('LARG')

But the word we want is 'large', isn't it?

So can you tell me what the Final Silent E is doing in the word 'large'? (FINAL SILENT E IS MAKING THE <G> SAY /J/)

This is the second part of job 2. Write it down.

JOB 2: Final Silent E makes <c> say /s/ and <g> say /j/.

NOTE: Final Silent E with two jobs

Now let's look at the word 'race'. What would this word sound like if you took the Final Silent E away? ('RAC', RHYMING WITH 'SACK')

But the word we want is 'race', isn't it? So can you tell me what Final Silent E is doing in the word 'race'? (FINAL SILENT E IS MAKING THE <A> SAY ITS NAME AND MAKING THE <C> SAY /S/)

In this word, Final Silent E is doing two jobs. It is such a powerful letter that it can do that. Another example is the word 'rage'.

What would this word sound like if you took away the Final Silent E? ('RAG')

But the word we want is 'rage', isn't it? So can you tell me what Final Silent E is doing in the word 'rage'? (FINAL SILENT E IS MAKING THE <A> SAY ITS NAME AND THE <G> SAY /J/)

In this word, Final Silent E is doing two jobs. It is such a powerful letter that it can do that. This should be noted. Let's write it down.

NOTE: Final Silent E can do two jobs at the same time.

Final Silent E Job 3

Let's take a look at the word 'due'. What would this word look and sound like if you took the Final Silent E away? ('DU/DUE')

It would sound the same, because we know that <u> at the end of a syllable will say its name. But what would be wrong with the word? (YOU MAY NOT USE THE LETTER U AT THE END OF A WORD. IT IS ILLEGAL. CHAPTER 13)

So how do you fix that when there is a /ue/ sound but you cannot have <u> at the end? (PUT A FINAL SILENT E ON THE END OF THE WORD)

Next we have 'give'. What would this word sound like if you took the Final Silent E away? ('GIV/GIVE')

It would sound the same, wouldn't it? But what would be wrong with the word? (YOU MAY NOT USE THE LETTER V AT THE END OF A WORD. IT IS ILLEGAL)

So how do you fix that when there is a /v/ sound but you cannot have <V> at the end? (PUT A FINAL SILENT E ON THE END OF THE WORD)

This is the next job. Write it down.

JOB 3: Final Silent E stops words from ending with Illegal Letters.

advice	circumference	evidence	increase	nose	rode	unfortunate
advise	circumstance	examine	injure	notice	rope	use
age	close	excuse	inside	oblige	rule	vague
alike	clothe	expense	interfere	occurrence	sacrifice	village
allege	coarse	experience	investigate	office	sale	voice
alone	college	exquisite	invite	once	same	volume
antique	combine	extreme	issue	one	scene	vote
apiece	compile	eye	judge	opportune	science	voyage
apologise	come	fake	June	orange	secure	waste
appreciate	commence	fame	justice	organise	seize	welfare
appropriate	compete	fare	knife	page	senate	were
approve	complete	fatigue	lace	palace	sense	where
architecture	comrade	favourite	lake	patience	sentence	while
argue	conference	feature	language	peace	separate	wire
arrange	consequence	female	large	perceive	serve	write
arrive	continue	fence	late	persevere	service	wrote
associate	courage	fertile	leave	persistence	severe	
assure	course	fierce	ledge	picture	share	
ate	creature	figure	leisure	piece	shine	
athlete	dance	file	license	place	shoe	
automobile	date	fine	lie	please	side	
avenue	debate	fire	life	pleasure	siege	
awe	deceive	five	like	police	since	
bake	deceptive	forgive	line	praise	sincere	
bare	decide	fortune	live	preference	size	
became	declare	freeze	lone	prepare	some	
because	describe	game	loose	preside	source	
become	desire	gave	lose	price	space	
before	desire	genuine	love	private	stole	
believe	die	give	mace	privilege	style	
beside	difference	gone	machine	race	suppose	
bone	distance	goose	made	raise	sure	
brace	distribute	grease	make	rate	surface	
brave	divide	have	male	realise	surprise	
breathe	done	here	marmalade	receive	table	
bridge	drive	hoarse	marriage	reference	take	
broke	due	hole	measure	refuse	telephone	
bruise	ease	home	mixture	rehearse	there	
cabbage	elaborate	illustrate	more	relate	therefore	
came	eliminate	image	mortgage	relative	these	
canoe	else	immediate	mouse	release	those	
capture	entrance	immense	name	relieve	tie	
care	envelope	importance	needle	resource	tire	
cheese	escape	impossible	niece	response	tissue	
choice	estate	improve	nice	reverence	tortoise	
choose	estimate	include	nine	ride	treasure	
	eve	income	none	rinse	twelve	
			nonsense	rite	twice	

Figure 16.5 Final Silent E wordlist

Final Silent E Jobs 1-3 spelling drill

1 time
2 judge
3 slice
4 brave
5 continue
6 relative
7 volume
8 wrote
9 improve
10 drive
11 fence
12 fringe
13 stole
14 image
15 choice
16 combine
17 glue
18 alone
19 forgive
20 since

17 Final Silent E, Job 4 (aka consonant plus -le)

There are many instances where Final Silent E goes together with a consonant and the letter <l> to form the final syllable of a word. For example, the word 'able' consists of two syllables. The first is the syllable a-. The second is the syllable -ble. As you can see, Final Silent E combined with the consonant <b> and the consonant <l> form the syllable -ble. The actual suffix is -le, but the preceding suffix can be analysed within the second morpheme. This then gives us an open/closed syllable distinction.

Operating rules

In this lesson, students learn and write the following rules:

RULE: Every syllable must have a vowel.
RULE: A consonant plus -le cannot be split up.

This helps them understand Job 4 of Final Silent E:

> JOB 4: Final Silent E can give the last syllable a vowel.

Lesson plan

Materials

Figure 17.2 Final Silent E Job 4 worksheet

Skill level

Job 4 requires more analysis than Jobs 1–3. Minimally, a student needs to have the following knowledge in order to get the best out of this lesson:

- Chapter 7: Counting syllables
- Chapter 10: The difference between vowels and consonants
- Chapter 14: The single vowels

Pattern

With the exception of <h> and <j>, all consonant plus -le endings that are crossed out have alternative spellings. This is shown on the completed worksheet in Figure 17.1.

Ending	Example 1	Example 2	Example 3	Example 4	Alternative spelling
-ble	able	babble	noble	hobble	cymbal, tubal, global, herbal, tribal, verbal, cannibal
-cle	cycle	uncle	article	icicle	logical, economical, alphabetical, vocal
-dle	idle	fiddle	ladle	paddle	pedal, bridal, feudal, medal, modal, scandal, tidal
-fle	sniffle	rifle			offal, duffel (also duffle), many words ending in the suffix -ful (wishful, wonderful, awful)
-gle	struggle	bugle	angle		fungal, legal, regal, madrigal, prodigal
-hle					
-jle					
-kle	ankle	sparkle	pickle	tackle	jackal (that's it!)
-lle					
-mle					normal, formal, camel, caramel
-nle					final, channel,
-ple	staple	apple	crumple	simple	opal, chapel, pupil
qle/qule					equal, sequel, tranquil
-rle					oral, squirrel, peril, petrol
-sle	hassle	tussle			
-stle	bristle	bustle	jostle	whistle	
-tle	title	little	startle	subtle	total, lintel, lentil, pistol
vle					oval, level, evil
wle					renewal, vowel
-xle	axle (that's all!)				
-zle	puzzle	drizzle	nozzle		bezel, pretzel, wurzel

Figure 17.1 Consonant plus -le example worksheet

Duration

This is a very dense lesson, with much scope for observation of several phenomena. 1–2 hours.

Step 1

Write all the consonants in the alphabet in the first column and add a dash (-) before each one and the letters ‹le› after.

Step 2

Return to -ble and dictate 'able'. Figure out what Final Silent E is doing in this word and write the rule in the first rule box:

RULE: Final Silent E can give the last syllable a vowel.

Step 3

Next to 'able', write 'babble'. Compare and discuss the single vs. double medial consonant in these words and brainstorm more examples. In so doing, the following rule emerges:

RULE: A consonant plus -le cannot be split up.

Step 4

Examine every consonant plus -le ending. Cross out the ones that don't exist and find examples for the ones that do.

Step 5

Depending on your students' tolerance of complexity, provide alternative spellings of the endings in the third column whilst looking at the consonant plus -le endings. If a simpler version is needed, go back to the beginning and look at the alternative spellings once all the consonant plus -le endings have been written.

Additional notes on Job 4

The suffix -al

The letters <al> form a suffix, used to denote adjectives from Latin, Greek, and English words ('final', 'original', 'total') or from nouns denoting verbal action ('arrival', 'burial', etc.).

When finding examples of consonant plus -le words, it is useful to have a column for alternative spellings there on the page. The worksheet reflects this.

Mispronunciation helps

Contrasting correct vs. incorrect pronunciation of the target words in this lesson is an engaging and memorable way of reinforcing the rules, e.g.:

TARGET WORD: 'idle'

If you were to spell 'idle' using two <d>s, so that the <i> in the first syllable was no longer in an open syllable, what would the word sound like? The answer is 'iddle', rhyming with 'fiddle'.

Conversely, 'fiddle' with one <d> would sound like 'fidle', rhyming with 'idle'.

-cle and -kle

These endings are a little bit different. Many other consonant plus -le words have single and double consonant counterparts ('idle/fiddle', 'apple/staple'). However, with -cle and -kle, there is no double-letter alternative (i.e. words in English do not end with -ccle or -kkle).

There are examples of -cle and -kle endings, such as in 'uncle', 'circle', and 'ankle', but they all have consonants which follow the vowel in the first syllable, thus closing the syllable and allowing the vowel to say its sound.

In two-syllable words, the final /kəl/ sounds are spelled with <ck>, such as 'buckle', 'tickle', 'tackle', and 'fickle'.

Words with more than two syllables

There are many 3+ syllable words where vowels are left in open syllables but no doubling occurs ('article', 'icicle', 'pinnacle', and 'chronicle'). This is a product of word emphasis being on a closed syllable, as underlined below:

article
icicle
pinnacle
chronicle

The vowel in the non-stressed, open syllable in each word becomes a weak, unstressed vowel sound called *schwa*. See Chapter 23.

Notes on unusual consonant plus -le endings

-lle

There are plenty of words ending with -lle ('belle', 'braille', 'gazelle'), a common French borrowing. However, please bear in mind that we are looking for *syllabic* examples of consonant plus -le – that is, with Final Silent E doing its fourth job. This job is to give the final syllable a vowel at the visual level.

In 'belle', 'braille', and 'gazelle', there is already a clear vowel letter in each syllable. This, then, is not an example of a syllable formed using consonant plus -le.

-fle

One of the alternative spellings for this ending is the suffix -ful. The suffix -ful means 'full of, having the qualities of'.

-mle

This is the first non-possible consonant plus -le ending that has an alternative spelling, namely -mal or -mel in 'normal' and 'camel'.

-nle

Aside from -al suffix endings as in 'final' and 'communal', there are many scientific words ending with -nol, such as 'ethanol', 'polyphenol', etc. Please bear in mind that these scientific words place emphasis on the final syllable and so are not true examples of alternative spellings for -nle words.

-ple

A commonly misspelled example of this ending is 'people'. Students should know that 'people' has a silent <o> like in the word 'leopard'. A useful mnemonic here is: 'When people see a leopard they say o!' 'Onomatopoeia' and 'diarrhoea' also have this silent <o> (in non-American spelling). Feel free to work them into the mnemonic if you wish.

-sle

The words 'isle' and 'aisle' are common examples of words ending with silent <s> plus -le. In many accents of English, they are pronounced as one syllable, so my thought is that it is useful to learn those words in the context of a word family.

-tle

Many words ending with this combination are preceded by the letter <s>. In most of these words, the <t> is left over from past times (e.g. 'castle' from Latin 'castra', meaning 'fort'; 'apostle' from Greek 'apostolos', meaning 'messenger', etc.)
Interestingly, the silent <t> still carries out the function of closing the first syllable.
    Here is a list of common -stle words:

    apostle, bristle, bustle, castle, epistle, jostle, rustle, thistle, whistle, wrestle

-vle

Watch out. Someone usually says 'revolve'. Just give them a minute to work it out.

-wle

There are no words which end this way in English, but there may be students who suggest alternative spellings in the form of 'renewal', 'dowel', 'trowel', etc. Whatever the answer, this is an interesting discussion point.
    In some accents, the <w> is pronounced very distinctly. In others, it collapses into the preceding vowel ('vowel' is an example of such a word). This forms a one-syllable word. This is an opportunity to resist *prescribing* a 'correct' pronunciation over enjoying and *describing* the variations.

-xle

'Axle' is the only example of this ending. Mysteriously, the preceding vowel is saying its sound, not its name. According to our rules, this word should be spelled 'axxle'.
    Here we have an interesting example of the overlap between our visual and our auditory systems as they relate to print.

The letter <x> is pronounced as the two phonemes /k/ and /s/ when it is word-internal and word-final. It is as if the two phonemes, expressed as one letter, are sufficient to close the first syllable.

Example lesson

Distribute the consonant plus -le worksheet and write the letters <le> after each consonant.

The first line should look like this:

-ble

This is a very common word ending in English. When you see it in a word, what will it say? (-BLE)

Let's write the word 'able' in the example box.

In the word 'able', how many syllables do you hear? (TWO)

What is the first syllable? (A-)

What is the second syllable? (-BLE)

What would the word sound like if we took away the Final Silent E? ('ABLE')

That's right, it would sound the same, so Final Silent E is not changing the sound of anything here. Is it stopping the word from ending with an Illegal Letter? (NO)

That's right, so what would be wrong with the second syllable if we took away the Final Silent E? (IT WOULD HAVE NO VOWEL, AND EVERY SYLLABLE MUST HAVE A VOWEL)

We've seen this before, when examining the importance of vowels. Now it's time to write it down as a rule.

RULE: Every syllable must have a vowel.

So we can fix syllables that don't have a vowel by adding Final Silent E. This is the fourth job, write it down.

JOB 4: Final Silent E can give the last syllable a vowel.

Next to 'able', write 'babble'.

In 'babble', how many syllables do you hear? (TWO)

What is the first syllable? (BAB-)

What is the second syllable? (-BLE)

What would the word sound like if we took away the Final Silent E? ('BABBLE')

That's right, it would sound the same, so Final Silent E is not changing the sound of anything here.

Is it stopping the word from ending with an Illegal Letter? (NO)

That's right, so what would be wrong with the second syllable if we took away the Final Silent E? (EVERY SYLLABLE MUST HAVE A VOWEL)

So how would we fix that? (ADD FINAL SILENT E)

There is something else you should know about words like this.

The word 'able' has one <b>, but 'babble' has two <b>s together. Let's see why this is.

What is the first syllable in 'babble'? (BAB-)

What's the second syllable? (-BLE)

Now let's take one of those <b>s away. The second <b> belongs to the last syllable, so we can't take that away. The syllable -ble is a whole unit and can't be split up. That is the next rule. Write it down.

RULE: A consonant plus -le cannot be split up.

So let's take the first <b> away. What would that first syllable now sound like? ('BAY')

Why would it sound like that? (BECAUSE THE LETTER <A> WOULD BE AT THE END OF THE SYLLABLE AND THEREFORE WOULD SAY ITS NAME) (Chapter 14)

So what would that word sound like with just one <b>? ('BABLE', WHICH RHYMES WITH 'TABLE')

So we fix the problem by doubling the <b>. This is one of the main reasons why we have double consonants in some words and single consonants in others.

Repeat for endings -cle, -dle, -fle, and -gle until you get to -hle.

When you get to the letter <h>, follow the procedure up to the point where the student writes -hle. Repeat for the rest of the endings, legal and illegal.

In English, you do not see these three letters at the end of a word. This is not a legal ending. Therefore, I would like you to cross it out.

There are some other illegal endings like this. Your job is to work out which ones are legal and which ones are illegal. For all the legal ones, you are to provide an example. Cross out all the illegal ones.

Optional section, depending on student ability

There are other ways to spell the /bəl/ sound in words. Does anyone know of any? Let's write some examples in the last column.

Ending	Example 1	Example 2	Example 3	Example 4	Alternative spelling
-b					
-c					
-d					
-f					
-g					
-h					
-j					
-k					

Figure 17.2 Consonant plus -le blank worksheet

Ending	Example 1	Example 2	Example 3	Example 4	Alternative spelling
-l					
-m					
-n					
-p					
-q					
-r					
-s					
-t					
-v					
-w					

Figure 17.2 Continued

Ending	Example 1	Example 2	Example 3	Example 4	Alternative spelling
-x					
-y					
-z					

Figure 17.2 Continued

Consonant plus -le words

-ble

able, affable, amble, amicable, answerable, arable, assemble, audible, available, babble, bible, cable, capable, charitable, comfortable, compatible, constable, couple, crumble, dabble, double, dribble, durable, edible, eligible, fable, feeble, flammable, formidable, fumble, gable, gamble, gobble, grumble, gullible, hobble, horrible, humble, impossible, incredible, legible, marble, miserable, mumble, nibble, nimble, noble, parable, pebble, portable, possible, probable, profitable, rabble, reliable, resemble, responsible, rubble, scramble, scribble, sensible, sociable, soluble, stable, stubble, stumble, syllable, table, terrible, thimble, treble (this and 'triple' are the only common two-syllable words that break the doubling rule), tremble, trouble, tumble, valuable, variable, vegetable, visible, wobble
   alternative spellings: cymbal, cannibal, global, herbal, tribal, tubal, label, libel, rebel, gerbil, gambol, symbol

-cle

article, bicycle, chronicle, circle, cubicle, manacle, miracle, obstacle, oracle, particle, spectacle, tentacle, uncle, vehicle
   alternative spellings: local, critical, radical, classical, electrical ... (there are too many to include here)

-dle

bundle, candle, cradle, cuddle, dawdle, doodle, dwindle, fiddle, fondle, griddle, handle, huddle, hurdle, idle, kindle, ladle, middle, muddle, needle, paddle, peddle, poodle, puddle, riddle, saddle, swindle, waddle
   alternative spellings: bridal, feudal, medal, modal, nodal, pedal, sandal, scandal, suicidal, tidal, vandal, model, yodel, strudel, idol

-fle

baffle, muffle, ruffle, scuffle, stifle, trifle
   alternative spellings: offal, farfal, duffel, falafel, and all the myriad '-ful' words (see notes)

-gle

angle, bugle, dangle, eagle, gaggle, gargle, giggle, goggle, Google, gurgle, haggle, jungle, mingle, rectangle, shingle, single, smuggle, spangle, straggle, strangle, struggle, tangle, tingle, triangle, wriggle
   alternative spellings: algal, centrifugal, conjugal, frugal, illegal, madrigal, prodigal, bagel, googol, mogul

-kle

ankle, buckle, cackle, fickle, freckle, knuckle, pickle, prickle, sickle, sparkle, sprinkle, tackle, tinkle, trickle, twinkle, wrinkle
   alternative spellings: jackal, pumpernickel, snorkel, yokel

-ple

crumple, dapple, dimple, disciple, example, grapple, maple, people, pimple, pineapple, principle, purple, quadruple, ripple, rumple, sample, simple, steeple, supple, temple, topple, trample, triple

alternative spellings: municipal, Oedipal, opal, principal, chapel, gospel, scalpel, papal, pupal, student

-sle

hassle, measle, tousle, tussle

-tle (with silent ⟨t⟩)

apostle, bristle, bustle, castle, epistle, hustle, jostle, rustle, thistle, whistle, wrestle

-tle

battle, brittle, cattle, dismantle, entitle, nettle, rattle, shuttle, skittle, startle, subtle, little, turtle, whittle

alternative spellings: hospital, capital, total, metal, environmental, vital … (too many to mention), chattel, hostel, lintel, pastel, lentil, pistol, capitol

-xle

axle

alternative spelling: pixel

-zle

dazzle, drizzle, embezzle, nozzle, sizzle *alternative spellings:* bezel, hazel, pretzel, wurzel

Spellings for illegal consonant plus -le endings

Spelled ⟨m⟩ + vowel + ⟨l⟩

animal, normal, formal, mammal, minimal, thermal, optimal, dismal, primal, maximal, baptismal, infinitesimal, abysmal, camel, caramel, enamel, pommel, pummel

Spelled ⟨n⟩ + vowel + ⟨l⟩

national, final, personal, professional … (too many to list)

channel, colonel, charnel, cracknel, fennel, flannel, fontanel, funnel, gunnel, kennel, kernel, panel, personnel, petrel, runnel, sentinel, shrapnel, simnel

Spelled <q> + <u> + vowel + <l>

equal, sequel, prequel, jonquil, tranquil

Spelled <r> + vowel + <l>

general, several, central, natural (too many to list), apparel, barrel, cockerel, doggerel, dotterel, kestrel, mackerel, laurel, minstrel, mongrel, petrel, quarrel, scoundrel, sorrel, squirrel, timbrel, tumbrel, wastrel, peril, petrel, nostril, tendril, tumbril, petrol, carol

Spelled <v> + vowel + <l>

approval, arrival, festival, survival, rival, interval, removal, medieval, revival, neural, retrieval, oval, upheaval, carnival, primeval, adjectival, larval archival, level, travel, hovel, gravel, marvel, unravel, shovel, swivel, reel, marvel, shrivel, grovel, civil, evil, devil, anvil, weevil

Spelled <w> + vowel + <l>

avowal, bestowal, renewal, withdrawal, bowel, towel, jewel, vowel, trowel, dowel (though in many accents, the final syllable collapses into the preceding one, rendering the words one syllable shorter)

Consonant plus -le spelling drill

1 cuddle
2 trifle
3 dismantle
4 tremble
5 crumble
6 vocal
7 fable
8 axle
9 nozzle
10 bugle
11 cycle
12 visible
13 goggle
14 hurdle
15 castle
16 tinkle
17 stifle
18 single
19 staple

18 Final Silent E
Additional jobs

There are some more reasons why <e> appears at the end of words. So far we have had Final Silent E giving a pronunciation signal for preceding vowels and consonants (Jobs 1-3) and completing a final syllable (Job 4).

We have also touched on Final Silent E being there as a remnant of a pronunciation in the past (No Job E).

However, that doesn't account for all instances of Final Silent E. The following functions of this letter are more subtle, in that they require a higher understanding of grammar and phonolgy than the previous ones. In Jobs 1-4, you could simply take the Final Silent E away and immediately see what the word would look/sound like in its absence - not so much for these jobs.

Plural-cancellling E

Some words end with a /s/ sound, and might be confused with plurals without Final Silent E. There are some handy pairs that demonstrate this, and there are some words that have this convention despite not having a plural counterpart.

First the pairs:

averse   avers
carse   cars
copse   cops
curse   curs
dense   dens
diverse   divers
goose   goos
hearse   hears
moose   moos
please   pleas
tease   teas
tense   tens
lapse   laps

Then some common solo examples:

course	house	sense
corpse	nurse	tense
eclipse	pulse	verse
else	purse	worse
false	response	
horse	rinse	

Giving consonants a voice

Final Silent E can also act as a signal to make the final consonant a voiced, rather than an unvoiced, sound. Take these pairs:

teeth	teethe
breath	breathe
bath	bathe
cloth	clothe
loath	loathe

Then some common solo examples:

cleanse
house (the verb)

Then some where there is variation:

rinse (some say /rins/, some say /rinz/)

Function vs. content words

Most of the two-letter words in English are what's known as *function words*. These are words that carry grammatical information and show relationships between content words in sentences. Content words are nouns, verbs, adjectives, and adverbs, whereas pronouns, determiners, prepositions, conjunctions, particles, and auxiliary verbs tend to fall into the function category.

Final Silent E helps to distinguish function from content words in pairs such as the following:

by	bye
be	bee
or	ore
he	hee (as in 'hee hee' laughter – often misspelled as 'he he')

19 Final Silent E and suffixes

This chapter deals with the addition of suffixes to Final Silent E words.

There is a simpler version of the rule and students are often able to quote it. The simple version is, 'drop the <e> and add <i-n-g>'. This is a good starting point but does not account for the addition of other common suffixes.

This leads to frequent misspellings, such as 'easey' for 'easy', 'writeing' for 'writing', and 'nerveous' for 'nervous'.

Lesson plan

Skill level

- Chapter 8: Affixes
- Chapters 16, 17, and 18: Final Silent E
- Handwriting
- Phonemic awareness
- Middle-primary minimum vocabulary

Materials

Figure 19.1 Final Silent E and suffixes worksheet

Duration

60–120 minutes

Step 1

Distribute the Final Silent E and suffixes worksheet (Figure 19.1) and dictate the base words, providing definitions and checking for understanding where necessary:

hope, dance, rehearse, humble, active, large, white, like, double, courage
… and the suffixes:

-ing, -er, -al, -est, -ly, -er, -ish, -en, -y, -ous

Step 2

Return to the word 'hope' and check if you are adding a vowel suffix.

Step 3

Figure out how to write the new word.

Step 4

Write the rule: When adding a vowel suffix to a Final Silent E word, take away the Final Silent E.

Step 5

Repeat for the remaining words.

Notes

- In 'active/actively', the Final Silent E is stopping the base from ending with an Illegal Letter. However, the suffix begins with a consonant, therefore the Final Silent E remains. Reward students for spotting this.
- In 'courage/courageous', the Final Silent E is making the <g> say /j/. However, it must remain when adding the vowel suffix -ous, as it needs something to keep the <g> saying /j/. Other words which do this are 'outrageous', 'advantageous', 'noticeable'. Contrast them with deleted <e>: 'outragous', 'advantagous', 'noticable' (Figures 19.1 and 19.2).

Example lesson

Now we're going to write some base words and suffixes to see how we make the new words. Here they are …

  hope, dance, rehearse, humble, active, large, white, like, double, courage

… and the suffixes:

  -ing, -er, -al, -est, -ly, -er, -ish, -en, -y, -ous

What do you see at the end of the word 'hope'? (FINAL SILENT E)
  What is it doing in this word? (MAKING THE <O> SAY ITS NAME)
  Now we are going to add the suffix -ing. Is this a vowel or a consonant suffix? (A VOWEL SUFFIX)
  Write the new word in the second column and tell me what it is. ('HOPING')

Write 'hoping' on the board. Some may take away the Final Silent E, some may not. Whatever the response:

1 Work out how to spell the new words.

2 Write the rule.

Word	Suffix	New word

Rule:

Figure 19.1 Final Silent E and suffixes blank worksheet

1 Work out how to spell the new words.

2 Write the rule.

Word	Suffix	New word
hope	-ing	hoping
dance	-er	dancer
rehearse	-al	rehearsal
humble	-est	humblest
active	-ly	actively
large	-er	larger
white	-ish	whitish
like	-en	liken
double	-y	doubly
courage	-ous	courageous

> **Rule:** When adding a vowel suffix to a Final Silent E word, take away the Final Silent E.

Figure 19.2 Final Silent E and suffixes example worksheet

'Hoping' is written without an E. There is a reason for this. When you add a vowel suffix to a Final Silent E word, you take away the Final Silent E. It is no longer needed, and in spelling, we always try to keep it simple.

This is the next rule.

RULE: When adding a vowel suffix to a Final Silent E word, take away the Final Silent E.

What do you see at the end of the word 'dance'? (FINAL SILENT E)

What is it doing in this word? (MAKING THE <C> SAY /S/)

Now we are going to add a suffix. The suffix is -er. Is this a vowel or a consonant suffix? (A VOWEL SUFFIX).

Write down the new word and tell me what it is. ('DANCER')

Just as you would with any other Final Silent E word, you take away the Final Silent E when adding a vowel suffix. It just so happens that this vowel suffix begins with the letter <e>, so it looks like you haven't taken away the Final Silent E at all.

Now let's figure out the spelling of the remaining words.

20 The Wicked Sisters and other Wacky Rs

Before teaching this lesson, do make sure your students have learned all the sounds that single vowels can make (Chapter 14). There are other sounds and spellings that they should know about. In this lesson, we are going to look at what happens to a vowel when it comes before the letter <r>.

A common spelling mistake in polysyllablic words involves the erroneous placing of the digraph <er> in place of a single vowel. For example, 'investergate' for 'investigate'.

When a vowel comes before the letter <r>, its sound changes. It's as if the letter <r> makes the vowels go a bit 'wacky', hence the name of the chapter.

Following is a list of Wacky Rs and example words:

-ar c<u>ar</u>
-er h<u>er</u>
-ir st<u>ir</u>
-or f<u>or</u>
-ur t<u>ur</u>n

There is a story I use in my practice for younger students to help them remember <er>, <ir>, and <ur>, which, in many accents of English, sound the same. The story also helps to remind learners of their order of commonality. They are called The Wicked Sisters, and the story goes:

> This is the story of the three wicked sisters. They do such wicked deeds that when people hear about them they say 'Er! Ir! Ur!'.
>
> Sister number one even has a wicked name. It's Frogmelda (thank you, Harry Enfield!). People find it such a terrible name that they never utter it, referring to this sister only as 'her' (Figure 20.1).
>
> Sister two is often mistaken for a man, on account of her luxuriant handlebar moustache. When she goes into a shop, she is greeted not with, 'Can I help you, madam', but, 'Can I help you sir?' (Figure 20.2).
>
> Sister three is actually a werewolf. When the moon is full, her face gets covered in fur! (Figure 20.3).

Figure 20.1 The Wicked
Sisters: 'her'

Figure 20.2 The Wicked
Sisters: 'sir'

Figure 20.3 The Wicked
Sisters: 'fur'

NB: This story works better in non-rhotic accents of English, such as most English and Australian accents. Scottish, Cornish, Canadian, and American speakers can still use the lesson, but must bear in mind that a vowel plus <r> becomes two phonemes, the first of which is different from the original vowel sound. The term Wacky R, therefore, can still apply.

The lessons in this chapter will also benefit your students in the following ways:

- Students begin to expand their explicit vowel knowledge from single to two-letter vowels.
- Students begin to eliminate another common coping strategy (i.e. the insertion of -er into unfamiliar words).

Lesson plan

Skill level

- Handwriting
- Phonics
- Chapter 12: Round the blend
- Chapter 14: The single vowels

Materials

Figure 20.4 Wacky Rs worksheet

Duration

20 minutes per Wacky R.

There is no step-by-step lesson plan for the first part. The worksheet is self-explanatory.

Example lesson

Distribute the Wacky Rs worksheet (Figure 20.4).

> When the letter <r> comes after a vowel, it makes the vowel go a bit wacky. Do you know what the letter <a> says when the letter <r> comes after it? ('AR')
>   This is the next rule. Write it down.
>
>   RULE: When a vowel comes before <r>, it goes wacky.
>
> Let's use the Consonant Start and End Cards to generate examples of <ar> words.

> Repeat for <er>, <ir>, <or>, and <ur> and tell the Wicked Sister story if appropriate (which, personally, I deem appropriate for everybody).

Wicked Sisters spelling drill

1 hurt
2 herd
3 bar
4 turn
5 fern
6 stir
7 more
8 person
9 church
10 first
11 serve
12 charm
13 start
14 girl
15 order
16 artist
17 torn

More Wacky Rs

With the core Wacky Rs in place, this information can now be expanded to produce other spelling patterns. The addition of other letters to the original Wacky Rs can produce some interesting patterns. They are listed later in the chapter, with word families to illustrate. The families are not intended as an exhaustive list of all possible words bearing these

1 Add the letter <r> to each vowel and pronounce the new sound.

2 Use your Consonant Start and End Cards to make example words and write them in the boxes below.

a	
e	
i	
o	
u	

3 Write the Wacky R Rule:

4 Draw the Three Wicked Sisters.

Figure 20.4 Wacky Rs worksheet

letter clusters. Compilation of such lists I will leave to online lexicographers and hopefully to your students.

Lesson plan

Skill level

Consonant Start and End Cards

Materials

Figure 20.5 More Wacky Rs worksheet.

Duration

60-80 minutes.

Step 1

Distribute the More Wacky Rs worksheet. Write <ar> in the first square and check the sound (/ar/ as in 'car').

Step 2

Insert the letter <e> before the <ar> and, noting that it spells the word 'ear', figure out what sounds it can also make when inside words by using the Consonant Start and End Cards. Using the cards will derive three distinct word families:

EAR
BEAR
LEARN

Step 3

Sort the words generated.

Example lesson

> We just looked at the Wacky Rs, but there are some more patterns that we can generate. Let's go to the next worksheet.
> When we add <e> to <ar>, we create three possible sounds. First, we have the word 'ear', so that's the first new sound. Let's put that word in the first 'new sound' box. Use your Consonant Start and End Cards to figure out the other <ear> sounds.

1 Add the letter <e> to <ar> and pronounce the new sounds.

2 Use your Consonant Start and End Cards to make example words like BEAR, DEAR and HEARD.

		New sound	Examples
e+	ar=		
e+	ar=		
e+	ar=		

3 Start a new word family for uncommon -ear- sounds.

uncommon -ear-	

4 Add the letter <w> to <or> and pronounce the new sound.

5 Use your Consonant End Card to make example words like WORD.

		New sound	Examples
w+	or=		

6 Start a new word family for uncommon -wor- sounds.

uncommon -wor-	

7 Add the letter <w> to <ar> and pronounce the new sound.

8 Use your Consonant Start and End Cards to make example words like WAR.

		New sound	Examples
w+	ar=		

Figure 20.5 More Wacky Rs blank worksheet

Brainstorm this. If the students are using the cards alphabetically, at some point they will generate 'bear' and 'learn'. Along with 'ear', these words can be used as the heads of the three word families.

There is also a space provided for the uncommon sounds such as in 'heart'.

When we add <w> to <or>, the <or> often makes a Wicked Sister sound, for instance, 'word'. Let's use the Consonant Start and End Cards to find more words like 'word'.

When we add <w> to <ar>, the <ar> often makes an /or/ sound, for instance, 'war'. Let's use the Consonant Start and End Cards to find more words like 'war'.

Some word families

<e> + <ar> = BEAR, DEAR, and LEARN word families:

BEAR

wear, pear, tear, swear

DEAR

nuclear, appear, arrears, beard, year, bleary, clear, dear, dreary, fear, gear, hear, near, rear, sear, shear, smear, spear, tear, weary

HEARD

search, dearth, early, earn, earth, heard, hearse, pearl, earnest, rehearse, research, search, yearn

With three possible exceptions:

heart, hearth, hearken

If students suggest 'heart', 'hearth', or possibly even 'hearken', let them know that they are exceptional words (victims, in fact, of 'The Great Vowel Shift', see Appendix 4: Why not just make spelling simpler?). Their spelling survived their change in pronunciation.

The EAR and BEAR families can also be expanded to generate homophones, for instance, 'hear/here, dear/deer, shear/sheer' or 'bear/bare, pear/pare/pair'.

<w> + <or> = WORD words and WORE words:

WORM: word, work, world, worse, worship, worst, worth
WORE: worn, wort

With 'worry' standing all on its own, I daren't even put it into a category based on its sound, it's so varied I'd get crucified for even suggesting where it might belong. The broad variations are due to its unusual status of being composed of very fluid sounds. Say it in your accent, noting your students' pronunciations based on their accents and then leave it alone.
<w> + <ar> = WAR words:

award, ward, dwarf, warn, warm, reward, toward, sward, swarm, swarthy, thwart, warrant, warble, wardrobe, warp, warren, wart

Words that denote direction, such as 'westward', 'inward', 'downward', and 'forward', all contain 'ward', but they have emphasis on the first syllable. Therefore, in these words, <w> + <ar> + <d> are pronounced with a weak vowel sound in the second syllable. This is also a good opportunity to compile a word family.

More Wacky Rs spelling drill

1 dwarf
2 worst
3 pearl
4 spear
5 work
6 heart
7 swear
8 warp
9 worm
10 heard

Final Silent E and Wacky Rs

Final Silent E combines with the five Wacky Rs, <ar>, <er>, <ir>, <or>, and <ur>, and forms different sounds. When Final Silent E is combined with <or>, many accents of English don't have a vowel sound change (Scottish does). It is still valuable to observe the words that can be generated by the addition of Final Silent E to Wacky Rs.

Common words with these sounds can be grouped together and learned as a family. Another interesting pattern emerges during these exercises, in that while students use the Consonant Start and End Cards, they also become aware of rhyming words. For instance, the cards will yield words like 'bare/bear' but also 'lair', 'peer', 'tyre', and 'roar', which inevitably triggers questions about alternative spellings. This is why the 'alternatives' column is there.

With the <er> row, the small, common, and therefore orthographically irregular words 'there', 'where', and 'were' are also generated. Put these into a separate word family based on the feature -ere + uncommon sound, if they are not already known.

Lesson plan

Materials

Figure 20.6 Final Silent E and Wacky Rs worksheet.

Duration

60–80 minutes.

Example lesson

> When you add Final Silent E to <ar>, aside from being the word 'are', it makes the sound /air/, as in the word 'bare'. Write this word in the 'new sound' box. There is a group of words spelled this way. See how many you can find by using your Consonant Start Card and write them into your 'examples' box.
>
> Now say the sound /er/. Add Final Silent E. When you add Final Silent E to this Wacky R, the sound it makes is /ear/, as in the word 'here'. Write this word in the 'new sound' box. There is a group of words spelled this way. See how many you can find by using your Consonant Start Card and write them into your 'examples' box.
>
> You will also find words that sound the same but are spelled differently. Put them into the 'alternatives' column.
>
> Repeat for Final Silent E + <ir>, <or>, and <ur>.

Final Silent E and Wacky Rs spelling drill

1 tire
2 dare
3 desire
4 manure
5 tore
6 mere
7 cure
8 fare
9 here
10 bore

1 Add the letter <e> to <ar> and pronounce the new sounds.

2 Use your Consonant Start and End Cards to make example words like BEAR, DEAR and HEARD.

		New sound	Examples
e+	ar=	bear	tear
e+	ar=	dear	near, hear
e+	ar=	heard	learn, earth

3 Start a new word family for uncommon -ear- sounds.

uncommon -ear-	heart, hearth

4 Add the letter <w> to <or> and pronounce the new sound.

5 Use your Consonant End Card to make example words like WORD.

		New sound	Examples
w+	or=	word	worth, worship

6 Start a new word family for uncommon -wor- sounds.

uncommon -wor-	sword, worn

7 Add the letter <w> to <ar> and pronounce the new sound.

8 Use your Consonant Start and End Cards to make example words like WAR.

		New sound	Examples
w+	ar=	war	warm, warn

Figure 20.6 More Wacky Rs example worksheet

1 Add the letter <e> to each Wacky R and pronounce the new sound.

2 Use your Consonant Start and End Cards to make example words and write them in the boxes below.

3 Use your Consonant Start and End Cards to find examples of alternative spellings.

Wacky R	+e	New sound	Examples	Alternatives
ar				
er				
ir				
or				
ur				

Figure 20.7 Final Silent E and Wacky Rs blank worksheet

1 Add the letter <e> to each Wacky R and pronounce the new sound.

2 Use your Consonant Start and End Cards to make example words and write them in the boxes below.

3 Use your Consonant Start and End Cards to find examples of alternative spellings.

Wacky R	+e	New sound	Examples	Alternatives
ar	are	bare	care, dare, fare	fair
er	ere	here	mere	
ir	ire	dire	hire, mire, tire	tyre
or	ore	bore	core, fore, gore	for
ur	ure	cure	pure, mature	

Figure 20.8 Final Silent E and Wacky Rs example worksheet

21 The Vowel Generator

The Vowel Generator is a system for forming all the possible two-letter vowels in our language. When two letters combine to form one sound, they are called *digraphs*.

The Vowel Generator consists of the combination of the five vowels with other letters to form all the vowel digraphs in English. Amazingly enough, there are only three other letters that vowels combine with to make the entire array of digraphs.

NB: Vowels can also combine with the letter <h>, such as in the interjection words 'ah', 'eh', 'oh', and 'uh', but I have not included them as I don't consider them true digraphs. They are not generally used independently in the spelling of other English words.

Lesson plan

Materials

- A printout of a blank Vowel Generator grid (Figure 21.1).
- Students will need to have their Consonant Start and End Cards out on the desk (Chapter 12).

Skill level

- Chapter 14: The single vowels
- Consonant Start and End Cards
- Knowing The Spelling Formula (Chapter 9) is very useful here when figuring out longer words.

Duration

60–120 minutes.

Step 1

Distribute a blank Vowel Generator (Figure 21.1). Leave the first square blank and fill the first row and column with the five single vowels. Figure out the additional three letters (<r>, <w>, and <y>) and place them in the last squares of row 1.

Figure 21.1 Vowel Generator blank worksheet

Step 2

Combine the columns with the rows to generate possible and non-possible vowel digraphs. Write examples for the possible digraphs and strike out the squares for the non-possible digraphs.

Notes on uncommon combinations

‹aa›

Dutch-derived words like 'aardvark' and 'aardwolf' are really the only examples of this combination.

‹ae›

Greek-derived words can have this combination, such as 'encyclopaedia', but it's not a common English digraph. American spelling has almost completely done away with it, e.g. 'pediatrician', 'encyclopedia', etc. Your judgement is required here as to whether to include this in the grid. I tend not to include it during intervention, but by all means teach it to mainstream learners.

‹ao›

Some students will suggest 'aorta' as an ‹ao› example, and true enough, the ‹a› and ‹o› are adjacent in this word and similar words, but we are looking at digraphs: two letters, one sound. Taken syllable by syllable, 'aorta' looks like this: a or ta. The ‹a› and the ‹o› do not combine to form one sound. Instead, they constitute separate syllables. The same can be said for ‹eo›, ‹io›, and ‹ia› words ('geography, 'diode', 'mania').

‹eo›

In 'leopard' and 'people', we have a non-functional, silent ‹o›, but this is an uncommon combination in English. Far better to cross this square and learn the words with the following mnemonic:

When people see a leopard, they say 'o!'

‹uy›

'Guy' and 'buy' are common examples of this digraph. Whether you want to call this uncommon and learn the words as a word family or not is up to you.

Patterns

The ‹o› row

This is the only fully filled row. The letter ‹o› appears to be super-friendly, but on further investigation (e.g. looking down the ‹o› column), you will find that it combines with other letters, but only if it goes first.

The <e> column

If you are including <ae>, then you can have your students observe the fact that this is one of two completely filled columns. This raises questions and answers about the letter <e> and its commonality and flexibility. The <e> row is also very full.

The <r> column

This is also a full column. In many accents of English, <r> combines with each vowel to form a new sound. Rhotic accents (Scottish, Irish, Cornish, American, and Canadian) pronounce vowel + <r> as separate phonemes. But even in these accents, the vowel sound is changed by the addition of <r>. Compare the vowel in 'cat' to that in 'car', 'sit' to 'sir', 'but' to 'burr'.

The letter <y> (see Chapter 15)

In the debate about <y> being a vowel vs. consonant, there is more evidence of the status of <y> being dependent on the environment. We don't add <y> to the bottom row of the grid. If we did, we would generate nonsense, such as 'ya', 'ye', 'yi' combinations.

Example lesson

Distribute a blank Vowel Generator (Figure 21.1).
　Leave the first square blank and write all the vowels across the first row.
　Then ask your students to write all the vowels again down the first column.

We are going to figure out all the possible two-letter combinations of vowels. We will do that by filling in this grid. This is called The Vowel Generator, because it generates all the two-letter vowels in English.

　Letters which combine to form one sound are called *digraphs*. 'Di' means 'two' and 'graph' means 'written or drawn'.

　To generate all the digraphs, though, we need three more letters. There are three other letters that go with the vowels <a>, <e>, <i>, <o>, and <u> to spell vowel sounds. Does anyone know any of them?

Once your students have answered, if there are any left that you need to discover, fill in the blanks. The letters are <r>, <w>, and <y>.

Let's generate the first two-letter vowel. Starting with the first letter in the first column, the letter <a>, let's combine it with the first letter in the top row. This would give us the vowel combination <aa>. Is that a common vowel digraph in English? (NO)

In that case we won't include it in our store of digraphs. Put a line through the <aa> square.

Our next combination is what? (<AE>)

Common or not common? (NOT COMMON)

Next combination? (<AI>)

Common or not? (COMMON)

What sound? (/AY/, AS IN 'PLAY')

Write 'ai' in the next square of the grid, leaving some space for your example words.

Can you think of any words that have this combination? Let's use the Consonant Cards and see what we can come up with.

Write your examples in your notebooks in a word family with feature <ai>.

The words we can generate using our consonant cards are mainly one-syllable words. Let's take a few and add some prefixes and suffixes.

Let's do an example word that doesn't come up with the consonant cards. How about 'contain'?

We could add some suffixes to that word. What suffixes? (-ER, -ED, -ING, -S, -MENT)

Time for the next digraph:

<ao>, yes or no? (NO)

Put a line through the <ao> square.

	a	e	i	o	u	r	w	y
a			ai contain		au August	ar particularly	aw unlawful	ay maybe
e	ea streamers	ee disagree	ei received		eu European	er wonderfully	ew renewable	ey valley
i		ie believable				ir firstly		
o	oa coastal	oe oboe	oi rejoined	oo cookery	ou compound	or recording	ow crowded	oy enjoyable
u		ue value	ui pursuit			ur surprisingly		

Figure 21.2 Vowel Generator example worksheet

	a	e	i	o	u			
a								
e								
i								
o								
u								

Figure 21.3 Vowel Generator (partial)

Continue to fill in the grid. Figure 21.2 shows a completed Vowel Generator with some suggested words.

Vowel Generator single syllable example words

<ai> bail, bait, fail
<au> caul, daub, fault
<ar> card, carp, cart
<aw> brawl, crawl, drawl
<ay> day, bay, say
<ea> beam, seat, teal
<ee> feed, deep, heel
<ei> skein, feint, heir
<eu> feud, sleuth
<er> herd, berth, serf
<ew> blew, crew, drew
<ey> they, key, prey
<ie> died, cried, dried
<ir> bird, dirt, shirt
<oa> boat, boast, toast
<oe> toed, floes, foes

<oi> boil, soil, toil
<oo> soot, hoot, boot
<ou> hound, south, mouth
<or> born, cord, forth
<ow> howl, down, flown
<oy> boy, joy, toy
<ue> blue, true, glue
<ui> fruit, suit, build
<ur> church, turn, churn

Vowel Generator spelling drill

It is useful to use the syllable lines per The Spelling Formula for words they are not sure of. Give them plenty of time to work out their answers.

1 party
2 server
3 goodness
4 sounding
5 never
6 sailboat
7 easy
8 reaching
9 floating
10 thousands
11 weather
12 ready
13 flowers
14 blueness
15 beater
16 sleepy
17 maybe
18 increased
19 cookery
20 compound
21 western
22 joyfully

22 Strong and weak syllables

Identifying, counting, and splitting words into syllables is common practice when learning to read and write. This is often as far as syllable study goes. This lesson is about going further.

Syllable patterns are also rule-based, and it is our knowledge of these rules that helps us understand meter in poetry and how words are manipulated to produce various effects in speech and writing.

The basic principle in this lesson, therefore, is that not only can words be split into syllables, but also those syllables have different strengths which vary from word to word.

For example, in the word 'banana', the vowel in the second syllable sounds much clearer than the vowels in the first and third, yet all syllables contain the letter <a>.

In the first and third syllables, <a> is making a weak, neutral sound. This sound is called *schwa*. In phonetic notation, it looks like this /ə/. Many English dictionaries transcribe the neutral vowel in weak syllables this way.

The schwa sound appears in 'banana' because the first and third syllables are weak and the second syllable is strong. We need strong and weak syllables in words, otherwise our speech would be monotonous and inexpressive and would require unnecessary effort.

Try saying 'banana' with strong /a/ sounds in every syllable. How does it sound? Does it feel right?

Schwa is defined as a mid-central vowel. The term 'mid-central' refers to the position of the articulators during this sound. Relatively speaking, they are 'at rest'. To use a motoring analogy, mid-central is like the neutral gear on a manual transmission.

Any vowel letter or letters can be represented as schwa in English if they occur in weak syllables.

Vowels in weak syllables are usually a schwa sound, but not always. In words of three or more syllables, vowels can also be quite clearly articulated in syllables other than the strongest one. This is called 'secondary stress' (not to be confused with teaching high school).

For example, 'maritime' has secondary stress in the third syllable and primary stress on the first. The vowels in both syllables are distinguishable, but the strongest, clearest vowel is the first.

We will come to a more in-depth study of schwa in the next chapter. The awareness of strong vs. weak syllables must come first.

If you like, you can test yourself on strong and weak syllables in words in the polysyllable wordlist at the end of this chapter. A good dictionary will also indicate strong syllables in its pronunciation guide.

Students should be encouraged to familiarise themselves with the pronunciation guide in their particular dictionaries as a matter of course. These guides do vary from dictionary to dictionary. For instance, the *Concise Oxford Dictionary* shows the strong syllable by placing a vertical bar directly after it:

/kul' prit/

Webster's and the *Scott Foresman* do the same. *The Chambers Children's Dictionary* makes the strong syllable appear in bold:

/**kul** prit/

> Not only can words be split into syllables, but also those syllables have different strengths which vary from word to word.

Strong syllable identification can be quite tricky, and many people have problems with this at first, but given enough practice and taught systematically, it can be mastered with relative ease.

The Anger Test

At a subconscious level, you already know where the strong and weak syllables are in all the words in your lexicon. Bringing that knowledge to the conscious level takes some practice. One way to do this is through dramatic, emotional enunciation.

Here's how it works: Pretend the target word is the operative word in a sentence that you are saying during an angry exchange. Let's start with 'banana'.

Say you're a toddler, just before nap-time perhaps, who requested a banana and was given an apple. In an angry voice, say 'I wanted a *banana*!'

Foot-stamping is optional, but certainly lends a kinaesthetic edge.

In the word 'banana', where was your voice loudest? In which syllable did you really snarl and channel your inner toddler?

Try this with as many words as you wish. You simply cannot help emphasising the strong syllable when being dramatic.

Sarcasm, surprise, and joy also work well when determining syllable emphasis.

Sarcasm: '*Oh great*, a banana.'
Surprise: 'Really? A banana?'
Joy: 'Fantastic! A banana!'

Do it wrong

When you can reliably identify strong and weak syllables using drama, try something a little harder. This time, see if you can deliberately stress the *wrong* syllable.

Let's take 'banana' again. We're all agreed that syllable two is the strong one. Now we're going to do two things to mispronounce it:

1 Consciously make the <a> in the first syllable clear and strong, as in 'cat'.
2 Consciously make the schwa sound /ə/ in the second syllable.

How did that feel? How did it sound? Non-native speakers of English have internalised syllable emphasis rules in their own language and sometimes apply these to English words. This is one of the ways in which we unconsciously identify non-native accents.

Practising incorrect emphasis helps you deliver precise auditory feedback to your students, so don't underestimate the power of this ability.

There is a wordlist of from two to five syllables at the end of this chapter (Figure 22.2), showing the strong syllable in bold for your reference.

Lesson plan

Skill level

Chapter 7: Counting syllables.

Materials

Figure 22.1 Strong and weak syllables worksheet.

Pattern

Strong syllables usually fall on the base element. Prefixes and suffixes tend to be de-emphasised.

Error pattern

Omission of a vowel in a weak syllable because it cannot be heard.

Duration

30–60 minutes.

Step 1

Distribute the strong syllables worksheet and use strong emotion and incorrect emphasis to determine the strong syllables in each target word.

Step 2

Underline the strong syllable in each target word and write the rule:
    In words with more than one syllable, there is always a strong syllable.

1 Underline the strong syllable in the words below.

button	adapt	respect
computer	animal	elephant
remembering	available	entertainment
immediately	manufacturing	organisation

2 Write the rule.

_____

_____

_____

_____

_____

3 How does your dictionary show strong syllables?

_____

_____

_____

_____

_____

Figure 22.1 Strong and weak syllables worksheet

Step 3

Look through your various classroom dictionaries and observe how syllable emphasis is indicated.

Example lesson

Distribute the strong syllables worksheet (Figure 22.1).

Can you tell me how many syllables are in the word 'button'? (TWO)

Now I want you to say the word and tell me which syllable sounds stronger. A good way to test for this is to shout the word as if you're angry. Let's try saying, 'Sew up that button!'

In 'button', which syllable was louder, longer, and clearer? (THE FIRST)

Give students the freedom to shout the word. This makes the lesson fun, but also teaches an important method of determining strong and weak syllables.

Handle any errors by exaggerating the syllable they chose as the strong one. For instance, 'button' would sound strange if we were to pronounce it 'butTON'.

To show that the first syllable is stronger, underline it. You have now shown which syllable is strong and which syllable is weak in the word 'button'.

All words of more than one syllable have strong and weak syllables in them. If this weren't true, our speech would sound boring and robotic.

Say this sentence without varying the tone of your voice so that you sound like a robot. This demonstrates the importance of strong and weak syllables.

This is the next rule. Let's write it down.

RULE: In a word with more than one syllable, there is always a strong syllable.

Let's see how our dictionaries show the strong syllable in words.

2 syllables	3 syllables	4 syllables	5 syllables
about	addition	application	accommodation
across	afternoon	atmospheric	antagonistic
after	animal	available	similarity
alone	another	calculation	appreciative
along	anything	celebration	specifically
apple	anyway	ceremony	argumentative
around	beautiful	circumference	superintendent
author	beginning	colonial	association
baby	company	combination	characteristic
became	computer	community	civilisation
behind	confusion	companionship	communication
belong	connection	comparison	congratulations
better	December	conventional	consideration
between	department	dictionary	continuation
brother	direction	difficulty	conversational
cannot	election	disagreement	curiosity
delay	employment	discovery	decomposition
dinner	estimate	distribution	determination
even	everything	education	environmental
female	family	elaborate	equatorial
finish	gentleman	entertainment	examination
forget	history	establishment	experimental
forgot	holiday	everybody	familiarity
Friday	however	exceptional	geometrical
happy	important	experience	horizontally
inside	nautical	favourable	imagination
letter	newspaper	generally	inactivity
maybe	nobody	identify	indigestible
Monday	November	illustration	individual
never	objection	impossible	investigation
only	October	inheritance	manufacturing
other	officer	interference	miscellaneous
outside	passenger	investigate	observatory
paper	permission	January	occasionally
party	personal	material	oppositional
report	position	necessary	ordinarily
river	president	particular	organisation
seven	primary	political	originated
sister	property	population	perpendicular
Sunday	regular	publication	personality
supper	relative	respectfully	popularity
today	remember	responsible	preliminary
twenty	represent	stationary	qualification
under	Saturday	stationery	satisfactory
water	September	television	university
winter	understand	testimony	unprofessional
without	vegetable	understanding	victoriously
yellow	violin	unfortunate	xenophobia

Figure 22.2 Strong and weak syllables wordlist

23 Schwa

Imagine only being able to hear 50% of the vowels in polysyllablic words and then being expected to spell those words correctly.

Is this the experience of the hearing impaired? Of those with phonological awareness deficits? Learning difficulties? No. This is the experience of many primary school students when they hear *schwa* (the unstressed, mid-central vowel common in weak syllables).

A variety of strategies emerges:

(a) Students with extensive sight word vocabularies make educated attempts, with an increasing degree of accuracy as more and more words are acquired in the mental lexicon.

(b) Students develop and use their own approximate vowel based on the pronunciation that most closely resembles schwa, according to their accent (/uh/, /er/, /i/, etc.).

(c) Students omit schwa letters altogether, leaving syllables with no vowels.

In the absence of explicit teaching, students who develop strategy (a) are most likely to become proficient spellers. Strategies (b) and (c) can lead to a downward spiral of word-avoidance and even abandonment of attempting to spell correctly at all.

In the preceding lesson, the notion of schwa was introduced. This lesson is to help teach it to your students.

The main points of this lesson are:

- That the vowel in the weak syllable is often schwa;
- That when schwa is heard, the most likely way to spell it is with a single vowel.

Schwa is pronounced as a relaxed, unrounded vowel. The articulators (tongue, jaw, and lips) are in their rest position. It takes minimum effort to pronounce this vowel, which is the entire point of its existence.

When talking, pronouncing every vowel clearly would take too much effort. We are economical with our breath and our time when we communicate. Emphasis on every vowel in every syllable would violate this necessary rule of economy.

This renders the vowels in the majority of syllables unidentifiable by auditory means. Put another way, people in the midst of developing the store of words that they can spell (as opposed to mature spellers) cannot *hear* the vowels in many of the syllables they have to write.

Knowing that the schwa sound exists and understanding the commonality scale of likely vowel letters is one strategy that helps take the guesswork out of spelling.

Schwa is probably the most common non-alphabetic sound-symbol we have, being present in pronunciation guides in many modern dictionaries. It is useful to know what it means and does.

> The vowel in the weak syllable is often /ə/, schwa.

The scale goes something like this:

MOST COMMON:	a/e (in roughly equal measure)
	i
	o
LEAST COMMON	u

Handily enough, they follow the order of the alphabet.

Lesson plan

Skill level

- Chapter 7: Counting syllables
- Chapter 22: Strong and weak syllables

Materials

Figure 23.2 Schwa worksheet

Pattern

Schwa vowels are most often written as single vowels.

Error pattern

- Omitting vowels from syllables
- Habitually writing two letters for schwa sounds

Duration

30–60 minutes.

Step 1

Take the words from the strong/weak syllables lesson ('button', 'adapt', 'respect'). Focus on the vowels in the weak syllables.

1 Rewrite the following words, underlining the strong syllable and replacing the single vowel with schwa.

button	adapt	respect
butt<u>ən</u>	ə<u>dapt</u>	rə<u>spect</u>

Write the rule:

The vowel in the weak syllable is often /ə/.

2 Rewrite the following words, replacing the schwa symbol with the correct single vowel.

Write the rule:

Schwa can replace any single vowel in a word.

2 Syllables	3 Syllables
1 əlive	1 princəpəl
alive	principal
2 bəcause	2 bəginning
because	beginning
3 lettəce	3 kangəroo
lettuce	kangaroo
4 listən	4 tragədy
listen	tragedy
5 persən	5 presənt
person	present

TALLY BOXES 2 & 3 SYLLABLE WORDS

a	e	i	o	u
iii	iiii	i	i	i
3	5	1	1	1

Figure 23.1 Schwa example worksheet

4 Syllables	5 Syllables
1 appləcatiən	1 argumentətive
application	argumentative
2 diffəcəlty	2 equətoriəl
difficulty	equatorial
3 əstablishmənt	3 əmalgəmatiən
establishment	amalgamation
4 teləvisiən	4 əxperəmentəl
television	experimental
5 ənherətənce	5 unəversəty
inheritance	university

TALLY BOXES 4 & 5 SYLLABLE WORDS

a	e	i	o	u
~~iiii~~ii	iiii	~~iiii~~ii	ii	i
7	4	7	2	1

Total vowel count

10	9	8	3	2

3 Complete this sentence:

When you hear schwa, try the single vowels first, in this order:

1. a
2. e
3. i
4. o
5. u

Figure 23.1 Continued

Step 2

Rewrite the words using the schwa symbol /ə/.

1 Rewrite the following words, underlining the strong syllable and replacing the single vowel with schwa.

button	adapt	respect

Write the rule:

2 Rewrite the following words, replacing the schwa symbol with the correct single vowel.

Write the rule:

Figure 23.2 Schwa blank worksheet

2 Syllables	3 Syllables
1 əlive	1 princəpəl
2 bəcause	2 bəginning
3 lettəce	3 kangəroo
4 listən	4 tragədy
5 persən	5 presənt

TALLY BOXES 2 & 3 SYLLABLE WORDS

a	e	i	o	u

Figure 23.2 Continued

4 Syllables	5 Syllables
6 appləcatiən	6 argumentətive
7 diffəcəlty	7 equətoriəl
8 əstablishmənt	8 əmalgəmatiən
9 teləvisiən	9 əxperəmentəl
10 ənheritənce	10 unəversəty

TALLY BOXES 4 & 5 SYLLABLE WORDS

a	e	i	o	u

Figure 23.2 Continued

Total vowel count

3 Complete this sentence:

When you hear schwa, try the single vowels first, in this order:

1 ___

2 ___

3 ___

4 ___

5 ___

Figure 23.2 Continued

Step 3

Write the rule:

The vowel in the weak syllable is often /ə/.

Step 4

Use the schwa worksheet to fill in and tally the vowels in the example words. Use this information to complete the sentence:
    When you hear schwa, try the single vowels first, in this order:

1

2

3

4

5

Example lesson

Now let's look at the word 'button' again. How many syllables are in this word? (TWO)
    And which one is the strong syllable? (THE FIRST, BUT-)
    In the first, strong syllable, what sound does the vowel make? (/U/ AS IN 'GUM')
    In the second, weak syllable, what sound does the vowel make?

Acknowledge any answers from students except if they say /o/ as in 'got'. Possible correct answers range from /er/ to /u/ and may even be /i/. This is okay, as long as students realise that even though there is a letter <o> here, it does not make either of the common sounds of this letter.

Because it is in a weak syllable, the vowel is less clear and strong.
    Some dictionaries write this weak vowel like an upside-down <e>, which is the symbol we are going to use. It is called schwa.
    In your worksheet, rewrite the word 'button', underlining the strong syllable and using the schwa symbol, for the letter <o> in the word.
    Now we're going to find schwa in some other words. Say this word: 'adapt'. How many syllables are in this word? (TWO)
    And which one is the strong syllable? (THE SECOND, -DAPT)
    In the second, strong syllable, what sound does the vowel make? (THE SOUND /A/ AS IN 'BAT')
    In the first, weak syllable, what sound does the vowel make? (/ə/)

Because it is in a weak syllable, the vowel is less clear and strong. When you hear an unclear, weak vowel like that, you know that you have a weak syllable. The vowel in this syllable in this word is called schwa.

Write the word 'adapt', underline the strong syllable, and write a schwa for the vowel in the weak syllable.

Now write the word 'respect' and put schwa in the right place.

Here is the rule, let's write it down:

RULE: The vowel in the weak syllable is often /ə/, schwa.

Schwa can replace any vowel in a word. Let's look at some words to see how this is true.

To show how schwa can replace the letter <a>, we are going to use the example word 'alive'. How many syllables are in this word? (TWO)

Which syllable is the strong syllable? (THE SECOND, -LIVE)

When you say this word naturally, what sound does the vowel in the first syllable make? (SCHWA)

Accept schwa sounds; do not accept /a/ as in 'cat'. We do not make this sound in the word 'alive'. Compare it to the first syllable in the word 'actor'. Same letter, very different sound.

Write the word 'alive', but put schwa in the first syllable. Underline the strong syllable, -live.

Schwa usually replaces a single vowel in a word. So when you hear the schwa sound, you will know that most of the time you have to choose between <a>, <e>, <i>, <o>, or <u> to spell the vowel. This is the next rule. Write it down:

RULE: Schwa can replace any single vowel in a word.

To help you choose between <a>, <e>, <i>, <o>, or <u>, we are going to look at how common each vowel is. Which do you think is the most common?

Tally the vowels which correspond to schwa in the example words and write the totals.
Finish the sentence 'When you hear …'

24 To double or not to double?

That is the question. Where do you use double consonants? Where do you only use a single consonant? Why is this?

A good speller with a large sight word vocabulary is a very efficient doubler.

Our first doubling lesson, 'Last 3 CVC', requires that students construct a table showing what happens when you add a vowel suffix to a particular type of word. The type of word we are looking for is one in which the last three letters fit the pattern 'consonant-vowel-consonant'. This is known as 'Last 3 CVC' for short.

The completed table is shown in Figure 24.1. The CVC columns establish whether or not the last three letters fit the CVC pattern.

Lesson plan

Skill level

- Chapter 7: Counting syllables
- Chapter 8: Affixes
- Chapter 10: The difference between vowels and consonants

Materials

Figure 24.2 Last 3 CVC blank worksheet.

Duration

60–120 minutes.

Step 1

Distribute the Last 3 CVC worksheet and dictate 'hop' for the first word.

Step 2

Use the Last 3 CVC column to count and tick the last three letters (sometimes they are the only letters, but as the words get bigger, keep orienting students to the last three letters).

WORD	LAST 3?			VOWEL SUFFIX?	✓	NEW WORD
	C	V	C			
hop	✓	✓	✓	-ing	✓	hopping
big	✓	✓	✓	-er	✓	bigger
stop	✓	✓	✓	-ed	✓	stopped
fit	✓	✓	✓	-est	✓	fittest
flat	✓	✓	✓	-en	✓	flatten
flat	✓	✓	✓	-ly	✗	flatly
neat	✗	✓	✓	-er	✓	neater
red	✓	✓	✓	-ish	✓	reddish
tight	✗	✗	✓	-en	✓	tighten
blast	✗	✗	✓	-ing	✓	blasting
mud	✓	✓	✓	-y	✓	muddy

Figure 24.1 Last 3 CVC example worksheet

Step 3

If there are three ticks in the CVC boxes, call this a 'Last 3 CVC' word. Dictate the suffix -ing and check if it begins with a vowel. Tick the vowel suffix box. Tell students that when you add a vowel suffix to a Last 3 CVC word, you double the final consonant in the base.

Step 4

Write the rule:

When you add a vowel suffix to a Last 3 CVC word, you must double the final consonant in the base.

Step 5

Dictate the remaining bases …

> big, stop, fit, flat, flat (again),neat, red, tight, blast, mud

… and the remaining suffixes …

> -er, -ed, -est, -en, -ly, -er, -ish, -en, -ing, y

… and apply to form new words.

WORD	LAST 3?			VOWEL SUFFIX?	✓	NEW WORD
	C	V	C			

Figure 24.2 Last 3 CVC blank worksheet

Step 6

Review all words, making sure students can say why some consonants are doubled and others aren't.

Notes

The important thing is that students understand the two crucial elements in this rule:

1 Last three letters fit the Last 3 CVC pattern
2 Addition of a vowel suffix

This rule will not work if the suffix begins with a consonant.

It is important that the students also go through this process in the correct sequence, as you are about to set them work which relies on that sequence.

When you come to 'flat/flatly', there is no double consonant in the new word, as -ly is not a vowel suffix. This is where it is vitally important to know the *whole* rule, not just the Last 3 CVC part. Make sure your students understand this.

Here is a list of common *consonant* suffixes:

-ful, -less, -ly, -ment, -ness

The final consonant in any base element does not double when these suffixes are added ('sinful', 'hatless', 'sadly', 'shipment', 'madness').

When you get to 'neat/neatest', you also do not double the final consonant. This is because there are two vowels in the base, so the pattern is VVC.

In 'tight/tighten', the pattern is CCV.

In 'blast/blasting', there are two consonants at the end of the base, giving it a VCC pattern, so no doubling occurs.

'Mud/muddy' is straightforward if students remember that the letter <y> is a vowel in most cases, and therefore -y is a vowel suffix.

Example lesson

Now we are going to do some counting. In the word 'hop', I want you to look at the letter pattern. There are only three letters in that word, but when we come to other words, there might be more. The ones we're really interested in here are the last three. We are going to see if those three letters match the pattern 'consonant-vowel-consonant', or CVC for short.

What kind of letter is <h>? (A CONSONANT)
So far so good. Put a tick in the first box.
What kind of letter is <o>? (A VOWEL)
This matches the pattern in the second box, so put a tick under the V.
What kind of letter is <p>? (A CONSONANT)

Good. So make sure you put a tick under the C. Now we have the pattern Last 3 CVC. We have done the first part. Now to the second part.

Now we're going to add a suffix to this Last 3 CVC word. The suffix is -ing. Write this suffix next to 'hop'.

What is the new word? ('HOPPING')

What does this suffix start with, a vowel or a consonant? (A VOWEL)

So we will call it a vowel suffix.

When you add a vowel suffix to a Last 3 CVC word, you have to double the final consonant in the base. What is the final consonant in the base? (<P>)

So our new word will have a double <p>.

Next to 'hop', in the last column, write 'hopping'.

Write 'hopping' after students have attempted to write the word for themselves. Some may spell it with a double <p>, some may not. Whatever the response:

Hopping is spelled with a double <p>. The reason for this is that when you have a Last 3 CVC word and you add a vowel suffix, you must double the final consonant in the base. This is the next rule. Write it down:

RULE: When you add a vowel suffix to a Last 3 CVC word, you must double the final consonant in the base.

If you didn't double that final consonant and you added the vowel suffix -ing, this is the word you would get: 'hoping' (write the word).

How many syllables are in that word? (TWO)

Where would you break the word into those syllables? (AFTER THE <O> BECAUSE WE SHOULD ALWAYS TRY TO START A SYLLABLE WITH A CONSONANT)

The letter <o> would come at the end of the syllable and so what would it say? (ITS NAME)

Therefore, that word would say ...? ('HOPING')

And we need the word 'hopping'. So to stop the <o> from saying its name, we have to use another <p> to close the syllable. This is one of the major reasons why some words have a single consonant and some words have a double consonant.

Underneath 'hop', write the word 'big'.

Now we are going to do this process again with some more words.

The students should be getting the idea now, so begin to ask them for the rule rather than telling them.

Last 3 CVC words spelling drill

Use a blank Last 3 CVC words worksheet (Figure 24.2) to work out the spellings of these words if necessary.

1 gasping
2 darken
3 slipped
4 greatest
5 baggy
6 gripping
7 griping
8 sitter
9 dryly
10 shipment
11 fatter
12 kindest

When the final syllable is like a Last 3 CVC Word

In words where the final syllable is the strong syllable, it can be treated like a Last 3 CVC word. Therefore when adding a vowel suffix, the final consonant is doubled in the base, just as before.

Example: 'begin' has emphasis on the final syllable. The final syllable can be treated like a Last 3 CVC word in this case. When adding the vowel suffix -ing, the final consonant is doubled.

Students fill out a table and discuss the rules as in the preceding lesson.

Lesson plan

Skill level

- Chapter 5: Counting syllables
- Chapter 8: The difference between vowels and consonants
- Chapter 6: Affixes

Materials

Figure 24.3 Final syllable Last 3 CVC worksheet.

Duration

60–120 minutes.

Step 1

Dictate example words:

begin, control, excel, forgot, enter, occur, admit, profit, acquit, budget

WORD	LAST 3?			VOWEL SUFFIX?	✓	NEW WORD
	C	V	C			
be<u>gin</u>	✓	✓	✓	-ing	✓	beginning
con<u>trol</u>	✓	✓	✓	-able	✓	controllable
ex<u>cel</u>	✓	✓	✓	-ent	✓	excellent
for<u>got</u>	✓	✓	✓	-en	✓	forgotten
<u>en</u>ter	final syllable is weak			-ing	✓	entering
oc<u>cur</u>	✓	✓	✓	-ence	✓	occurrence
ad<u>mit</u>	✓	✓	✓	-ance	✓	admittance
<u>pro</u>fit	final syllable is weak			-able	✓	profitable
ac<u>quit</u>	✓	✓	✓	-al	✓	acquittal
<u>bud</u>get	final syllable is weak			-ed	✓	budgeted

Figure 24.3 Strong syllable CVC example worksheet

Step 2

Dictate suffixes:

   -ing, -able, -ent, -en, -ing, -ence, -ance, -able, -al, -ed

Step 3

Return to the word 'begin' and check which syllable is the strong syllable. If it is the final syllable, underline it and continue by counting the last three letters as before.

   If it goes Last 3 CVC, as in the words in the preceding lesson, then double the final consonant in the base when adding a vowel suffix. Write the new word in the last column.

Step 4

Write the rule:

RULE: When the final syllable
is strong and
acts like a Last 3 CVC word
double the final consonant in the base
when adding a vowel suffix.

WORD	LAST 3?			VOWEL SUFFIX?	✓	NEW WORD
	C	V	C			

Figure 24.4 Strong syllable CVC blank worksheet

Step 5

Repeat the process for the remaining bases and suffixes and review.

Notes

- 'Enter/entering' does not use the rule because the strong syllable is not the final syllable. Students need go no further in identifying the different parts of this word once they have established that the strong syllable is not the final syllable.
- 'Profit/profitable' does not use the rule because the strong syllable is not the final syllable.
- 'Budget/budgeted' does not use the rule because the strong syllable is not the final syllable.

Example lesson

In the word 'begin', which is the strong syllable? (-GIN)

Mark the strong syllable by underlining it. If that final syllable is strong, then we can go on. If it isn't, then just add the suffix without changing anything.

We are going to add a suffix, like we did last time, but first we have to find some things out.

What is the letter pattern in the final syllable? (LAST 3 CVC)

Make sure you tick the boxes just like last time.

This strong syllable acts just like a Last 3 CVC word. So when we add a vowel suffix, like -ing, what do you think we do with the final consonant? (WE DOUBLE IT)

Now write the suffix -ing in the next column and the new word 'beginning' in the last column.

So now that you have this example, can you work out what the next rule is? It comes in three parts. Here it is:

RULE: When the final syllable is:

1 Strong and
2 Acts like a Last 3 CVC word

double the final consonant when adding a vowel suffix.

Final syllable/Last 3 CVC word spelling drill

1 belonging
2 forgotten
3 dusty
4 compelled
5 embedding
6 unplanned
7 babysitter
8 transmitted
9 plumpest

25 The return of Illegal <i>

A common partial rule relating to how word-final <y> changes is the saying, 'Drop the <y>, add <ies>'. This explains why 'cry' becomes 'cries', 'party' becomes 'parties', etc.

This is useful for addition of the suffix -s, but not much else.

It is far more useful to bring back the concept of <y> and <i> being interchangeable, with <y> going where <i> may not (see Chapter 15: The letter <y>).

Adding a suffix to a word-final <y> word transports this vowel from being in a word-final to a word-internal position, thus negating its existence as a 'stunt letter'. It is then free to return to its regular form and becomes <i> again.

This rule operates during the addition of both vowel *and* consonant suffixes.

Adding -s/-es

The letter <s> is a suffix which denotes plurals and verbs in the third person singular. For clarity, the letter <e> is inserted between the returned <i> and the <s>, as in 'cry/cries'. Without the inserted <e>, the inflected form would read 'cris' rhyming with 'miss', since there would be no reason for the <i> to say its name. Even in words like 'city', where the final vowel is more /ee/-like, the insertion of <e> after returned <i> helps retain that /ee/ sound – compare 'cities' with 'citis'.

Adding -th/-eth

An inserted <e> is also required when converting cardinal numbers to their ordinal form, e.g. 'twenty/twentieth', 'fifty/fiftieth'. This is also an aid to pronunciation – compare saying 'twentieth' and 'twentith'.

Lesson plan

Skill level

- Chapter 8: Affixes
- Chapter 13: Illegal Letters
- Chapter 21: The Vowel Generator

Materials

Figure 25.1 Return of Illegal <i> worksheet.

1 Write the base words and the suffixes.

2 Write the new words.

3 Write the rules.

Word	Suffix	New word

Rule: When adding a suffix to word-final <y>

_____

_____

_____

Rule: _____

_____

_____

Figure 25.1 Return of Illegal <i> blank worksheet

Duration

60–120 minutes.

Step 1

Distribute return of Illegal <i> worksheet (Figure 25.1) and dictate the base words:

angry, fifty, party, happy, twenty, cry, funny, lady, library, many, naughty

1 Write the base words and the suffixes.

2 Write the new words.

3 Write the rules.

Word	Suffix	New word
angry	-ly	angrily
fifty	-th	fiftieth
party	-s	parties
happy	-ness	happiness
twenty	-th	twentieth
cry	-s	cries
funny	-er	funnier
lady	-s	ladies
library	-an	librarian
many	-fold	manifold
naughty	-ness	naughtiness

Rule: When adding a suffix to word-final 'y' return 'y' to 'i'
Rule: When returning 'y' to 'i' and adding the suffixes -th or -s, you must add 'e'.

Figure 25.2 Return of Illegal <i> example worksheet

… and the suffixes:

   -ly, -(e)th, (e)s, -ness, (e)th, (e)s, -er, (e)s, -an, -fold, -ness

The bracketed ‹e›s are not to be dictated, but are there as a reminder that these suffixes require the insertion of ‹e› when returning ‹y› to ‹i›.

Step 2

Go to the word 'angry'. Figure out what happens to word-final letter ‹y› when adding the suffix -ly. Write the new word, 'angrily' in the new column. Write the rule:

   RULE: When adding a suffix to a word-final ‹y› word, return ‹y› to ‹i›.

Step 3

Go to the next word, 'fifty'. Figure out what happens to word-final ‹y› when adding the suffix -th. This time it is not enough to simply replace the ‹y› with ‹i›. See if your students can explain what happens and why, by writing and saying the word without the ‹e›.

Step 4

When that is done, go to the next word 'party' and figure out what happens to ‹y› when the suffix -s is added.

Step 5

Write the new words, 'fiftieth' and 'parties', in the next column. Write the rule:

   RULE: When returning ‹y› to ‹i› and adding the suffixes -th or -s, you must add ‹e›.

Continue with the rest of the words, noting the new words that require insertion of ‹e›.

Example lesson

> We are going to add the suffix -ly to the word 'angry'. If we did this without changing anything, this is what the new word would look like: 'angryly'. How does that look to you? (IT LOOKS WRONG)
>
>   The reason for this is that unless we're spelling Greek-derived words, the letter ‹y› is only there to stand in for ‹i› or ‹e›. Let's take that apart.
>
>   Why does ‹y› go at the end of 'angry'? (BECAUSE ANY OTHER LETTER WOULD BE ILLEGAL)

> In 'angrily', we need an /i/ sound in the second syllable, but because there's a syl-
> lable right after it, we don't need to use the letter <y> any more. So Illegal <i> can return.
> That's why this lesson is called 'The return of Illegal i'.
>
> This works for the addition of vowel *and* consonant suffixes.
>
> There are times when returning Illegal <i> is not enough. When converting 'twenty'
> to 'twentieth', for instance, just returning Illegal <i> would result in this word: 'twentith'.
>
> What's wrong with that? (IT DOESN'T LOOK OR SOUND RIGHT)
>
> What's the solution? (INSERT <E> AFTER RETURNING ILLEGAL <I>)
>
> See if you can spot where we need to insert <e>.

Final Silent E and suffixes spelling drill

1 business
2 easier
3 ladies
4 dutiful
5 earliest
6 shakily
7 properties
8 mysterious

26 The Suffix Generator

Working with suffixes teaches students to process words right to the end.

In reading, if students are rewarded for guessing or 'having a go' at difficult words by way of initial letters, looking at illustrations, or using contextual cues, they run the risk of forming habits in place of processing each word from start to finish. This leads at first to an illusion of fluency, but actually it is a game of roulette, the odds becoming less advantageous as words become longer and less familiar.

A really helpful exercise, then, would be to teach the building blocks of words and say, 'read what is there'. The Suffix Generator teaches a great deal of those building blocks that can otherwise be, in isolation, confounding.

In my practice, I try not to let students get into or continue the habit of guessing what words are. That is not to say that good readers don't use context. They do this to figure out the meaning of words not already in their lexicon. But they can only do this after building an appropriately solid foundation of phonemic awareness and phonic knowledge. Good readers do not use context to identify new words. You cannot use pictures or guesswork to figure out a word you don't already know. Only letters will do that.

Poor readers often struggle because they lack this foundation. It is therefore cruel indeed to ask them to make an educated guess in the absence of education.

In spelling, The Suffix Generator also helps replace habits of guessing how words end by putting in place a set of predictable, organised suffixes.

Struggling spellers show difficulty in identifying word endings (Moats 1995) and often apply a coping strategy for word endings that goes something like this: 'If in doubt, add an <e>.' This lesson presents a much better way to end words.

The Lindamood Phoneme Sequencing (LiPS) Program, a world-class language arts instructional program with particular emphasis on the kinaesthetic aspect of sound production, refers to these suffixes in a much-expanded table called 'The Ending Grid'. This is well worth a look.

This lesson consists of a table of suffixes with notes on pronunciation and usage. This is a great opportunity to use The Spelling Formula (Chapter 9). At the very least, when students are figuring out their example words, they should draw syllable lines on which they can immediately place their suffixes.

> The Suffix Generator helps replace habits of guessing how words end by putting in place a set of predictable, organised suffixes.

Lesson plan

Skill level

- Chapter 7: Counting syllables
- Chapter 23: Schwa

Materials

Figure 26.1 Suffix Generator blank worksheet

Duration

60–120 minutes.

Step 1

Distribute the blank Suffix Generator and examine the operative rule in the first square of row 2:

Vowel = /ə/

Step 2

In the next square, write -a and pronounce the sound that it will make in the word-final position according to the operative rule (/ə/).

Step 3

Find three example words and write them in the grid or in notebooks, depending on how much space is needed. With older students, we play the '1, 2, 3 Game', where one point is awarded for a regular word, two points for a longer or irregular word, and three points for a very difficult word. In Figure 26.2 there are example words of increasing difficulty in each square.

Step 4

Generate the top row of suffixes, following the same pattern: asking for pronunciations and finding examples.

   Use suffixes -an, -on, -al, -ous, -ent, -ence.

   This is called the 'key row', from which all other suffixes and stable endings will be generated. The first two rows contain actual suffixes. The remaining rows contain those suffixes merged with consonants that come at the end of their bases. For example, the base 'magic' merges with the suffix -ian and the final consonant undergoes a change in pronunciation, moving from a /k/ to a /sh/ sound.

   The class of word each suffix typically denotes can be added in the top row.

Rule						
vowel = /ə/						
i = /ee/						
ti = /sh/						
ci = /sh/						

Figure 26.1 Suffix Generator blank worksheet

Rule	Nouns	Beings	Objects	Adjectives	Adjectives	Adjectives/Nouns	Nouns
vowel = /ə/	-a 1 banana 2 peninsula 3 propaganda	-an 1 human 2 hooligan 3 metropolitan	-on 1 bacon 2 gibbon 3 rhododendron	-al 1 final 2 immortal 3 unilateral	-ous 1 famous 2 generous 3 simultaneous	-ent 1 silent 2 accident 3 impertinent	-ence 1 sequence 2 eloquence 3 circumference
i = /ee/	-ia 1 phobia 2 insomnia 3 pneumonia	-ian 1 Indian 2. comedian 3 equestrian	-ion 1 scorpion 2 onion 3 communion	-ial 1 serial 2 marsupial 3 ceremonial	-ious 1 devious 2 amphibious 3 mysterious	-ient 1 gradient 2 obedient 3 inconvenient	-ience 1 audience 2 experience
ti = /sh/	-tia 1. militia 2. dementia 3. inertia	-tian 1 Martian 2 Dalmatian 3 Egyptian	-tion 1 station 2 precaution 3 repudiation	-tial 1 partial 2 sequential 3 influential	-tious 1 cautious 2 ambitious 3 confidential	-tient 1 patient 2 sentient	-tience 1 patience 2 sentience
ci = /sh/	-cia 1. Marcia 2. acacia 3. alopecia	-cian 1 magician 2 musician 3 physician	-cion 1 suspicion 2 coercion	-cial 1 facial 2 official 3 beneficial	-cious 1 vicious 2 ferocious 3 unconscious	-cient 1 ancient 2 deficient 3 sufficient	-cience 1 conscience

Figure 26.2 Suffix Generator example worksheet (adapted from Phyllis Lindamood, 'The Lindamood® Phoneme Sequencing Program', Lindamood-Bell)

Step 5

After generating the key row, ask if anyone has noticed a pattern in the type of word each suffix denotes. When you have figured this out, write the categories in the top row as shown in Figure 26.1.

In the second and third columns, both suffixes denote nouns, but those ending in -an are far more likely to refer to beings rather than objects, which tends to be the domain of the -on suffix. There are exceptions, of course ('tartan', 'toucan', 'Amazon', 'person', 'deacon').

Step 6

Go to the next row and write the operative rule <i> says /ee/. Combine the letter <i> with the suffixes generated in the key row, and a whole new batch of suffixes appears.

This is the only row that has a two-syllable suffix. When using The Spelling Formula, make sure the two syllables are represented properly with two separate lines.

Step 7

Repeat for rows 3 and 4.

Notes

Additional suffixes can be generated when adding <si> to -a, -an, and -on. A list of possible words is included in the wordlist for this chapter.

In the same way, <gi> can be added to -a, -an, -on, and -ous, also included in the wordlist.

Line 4: <ci> says /sh/

Why not spell everything with ti- and be done with it? It is useful here to look at the base of <ci> words and figure out why (i.e. they commonly end with the letter <c>, hence the direct conversion).

magic/magician
music/musician
face/facial
office/official

When I reach the -cience square, there is only one common word with this ending, that is, 'conscience'. It has a hidden letter <s> in it. In Chapter 6, Mnemonics, there is a lesson on teaching this word.

Ending Grid Bingo

A popular activity at Lifelong Literacy is to play Ending Grid Bingo. It's better with small groups so that answers can be checked quickly and the game doesn't lose pace.

A completed Suffix Generator is distributed (minus example words) and random example words are selected by the teacher (I have a box of laminated words I put together in about half an hour).

Students spell the words, check them, and if they're correct, they get to place a counter on the square to which the words belong. The first person with a completed column or row is the winner.

Example lesson

We are going to generate some suffixes using this grid. The first rule says:

Vowel = /ə/

This means that all the vowels in the suffixes in this row say /ə/.

The first vowel that we are going to deal with is ‹a›. At the end of a word, it says /ə/. Write it down with a hyphen to indicate the rest of the word.

Can you think of any words that follow this rule?

Acknowledge any suggestions. Students will often give words that start with this vowel. Correct this by directing them to the end of the word and saying, 'We are looking for that sound at the end of the word'.

Write 'banana' and any other example words students come up with. Let them work out the spelling as best they can before providing help.

Next to -a, write this suffix: -an. The rule says that the vowel will say /ə/ at the end of a word, so what will this suffix sound like? (/əN/)

Do you know any words with this ending? See if you can work out our example word. What type of being are you? (HUMAN)

Write this word in the box.

Next to -an, write this suffix: -on. The rule says that the vowel will say the schwa sound, so what will this suffix sound like?

Is that the same sound or a different sound to the ending that we had in the last box? (THE SAME)

Why is it the same? (BECAUSE THE RULE TELLS US THAT THE VOWEL SAYS /ə/)

Do you know any words with this ending? See if you can work out our example word. What is the salty breakfast food you eat with eggs? ('BACON')

Write this word in the box.

Row 2: ‹i› says /ee/

When you have completed the first row, say:

Now it is time for the next rule. Go to the next row. The rule is ‹i› = /ee/.

We are now going to combine the letter ‹i› with the suffixes on the top row, so what will your first suffix on this row look like? (-IA)
And what will it sound like? (/EE-ə/)
Write it down in the box. See if you can work out our example word. It is an irrational fear of something. ('PHOBIA')

Students will be very proud if they can spell this themselves when previously they thought they couldn't. Don't forget to use The Spelling Formula (Chapter 9) to work out the words and make sure your students know that this is a Greek-derived word.
Continue with the second row, etc.

Examples for The Suffix Generator

There are hundreds of other examples, I'm sure. Many have not been included because they are so common, such as words ending with ‹tion›. Others haven't made the list due to the fact that their rarity gives them very limited practical use.

Words ending in -a

Africa, America, amoeba, anaconda, antenna, aorta, area, arena, aroma, asthma, ballerina, balsa, banana, camera, Cleopatra, comma, delta, dilemma, diploma, dogma, Dracula, drama, enigma, fibula, flora, formula, gondola, gorilla, guerilla, gymkhana, hyena, idea, impala, influenza, iguana, lava, llama, nausea, opera, pagoda, panama, panda, panorama, peninsula, piranha, plasma, propaganda, puma, quota, replica, retina, rota, savanna, scuba, sofa, sonata, soya, stamina, stigma, spatula, tarantula, toga, tuba, tuna, tundra, umbrella, vanilla, veranda, viola, yoga, zebra

Words ending in -an

African, American, hooligan, human, metropolitan, organ, pagan, pelican, postman, Roman, slogan, tartan, urban, veteran, woman

Words ending in -on

abandon, Amazon, apron, arson, bacon, badminton, baton, beacon, bison, button, cannon, canyon, carbon, carton, chameleon, common, cotton, crimson, dragon, flagon, galleon, gallon, garrison, gibbon, glutton, heron, hexagon, horizon, imprison, jargon, jettison, lemon, lexicon, lion, London, mason, melon, mutton, nylon, octagon, pardon, patron, pentagon, person, phenomenon, piston, plankton, poison, prison, pylon, python, reason, reckon, rhododendron, ribbon, salmon, season, sermon, silicon, siphon, skeleton, Stetson, summon, surgeon, tendon, treason, wagon, weapon

Words ending in -al

abysmal, actual, admiral, animal, annual, brutal, capital, cardinal, carnival, casual, cathedral, central, centrifugal, cereal, chemical, classical, colossal, continual, coral, criminal, critical, crystal, cymbal, decimal, denial, dental, diagonal, dismal, dual, electrical, elliptical, ephemeral, Episcopal, equal, equilateral, eternal, ethical, eventual, external, factual, federal, feudal, final, formal, fraternal, frugal, fundamental, funeral, general, gradual, grammatical, horizontal, hospital, ideal, identical, illegal, illogical, immoral, immortal, impractical, incidental, individual, informal, internal, interval, irrational, journal, lateral, legal, lethal, local, loyal, mammal, manual, maternal, medal, medical, mental, metal, methodical, mineral, monumental, moral, mortal, mural, mutual, nasal, national, natural, nautical, neutral, nocturnal, normal, numeral, numerical, pedal, pedestal, personal, petal, phial, physical, plural, practical, primeval, principal, prodigal, punctual, quadrilateral, radical, rational, rehearsal, rural, ritual, rival, sandal, scandal, seasonal, sensational, sentimental, several, signal, spinal, spiral, spiritual, technical, terminal, total, typical, unequal, unilateral, usual, vandal, vertical, visual, vital, vocal

Words ending in -ous

ambidextrous, ambiguous, amorphous, anonymous, callous, conspicuous, continuous, courageous, courteous, deciduous, enormous, fabulous, famous, frivolous, generous, gorgeous, humorous, igneous, indigenous, infamous, jealous, ludicrous, miraculous, monotonous, monstrous, nervous, numerous, pious, poisonous, pompous, ponderous, ridiculous, simultaneous, strenuous, spontaneous, treacherous, tremendous, unanimous

Words ending in -ent

accent, accident, adjacent, adolescent, advertisement, affluent, agent, ailment, apparent, ardent, argument, basement, battlement, client, coherent, compartment, competent, complacent, complement, compliment, consistent, convalescent, continent, convent, crescent, current, department, despondent, detergent, diffident, diligent, dissident, document, effluent, element, embankment, eminent, employment, environment, equivalent, excellent, experiment, filament, fluent, fragment, garment, impertinent, implement, incident, incompetent, indifferent, innocent, insolent, instalment, instrument, intelligent, iridescent, ligament, magnificent, monument, ointment, opponent, ornament, parchment, parliament, pavement, pertinent, parent, patent, permanent, pigment, predicament, prudent, rodent, sediment, segment, sentiment, serpent, settlement, student, talent, testament, torrent, tournament, transparent, trident, translucent, violent

Words ending in -ence

absence, circumference, coincidence, conference, confidence, confluence, consequence, difference, eloquence, essence, evidence, influence, prominence, reference, residence, science, silence, sequence

Words ending in -ia

agoraphobia, ammonia, anaemia, anorexia, Australia, bacteria, dyslexia, encyclopaedia, hypochondria, hypothermia, hysteria, insignia, insomnia, magnolia, malaria, mania, media, phobia, pneumonia, trivia, utopia, via, xenophobia

Words ending in -ian

amphibian, Australian, barbarian, civilian, comedian, equestrian, historian, Indian, Italian, meridian, pedestrian, ruffian

Words ending in -ion

battalion, billion, carrion, champion, communion, companion, criterion, dominion, million, onion, opinion, pavilion, rebellion, reunion, scorpion, stallion, union

Words ending in -ial

aerial, biennial, ceremonial, colloquial, imperial, industrial, jovial, marsupial, material, memorial, serial, terrestrial, triennial

Words ending in -ious

amphibious, curious, devious, dubious, envious, furious, glorious, hilarious, ingenious, luxurious, mysterious, notorious, obvious, precarious, previous, serious, studious, tedious, various

Words ending in -ient

convenient, gradient, inconvenient, nutrient, obedient

Words ending in -ience

audience, experience, obedience

From this point onwards, the same suffixes appear again, but combined with the final consonant in their bases, a pronunciation change takes place. The units they form can be referred to as 'stable endings'.

Words ending in -tia

dementia, inertia, militia

Words ending in -tian

Dalmatian, Egyptian, Martian

Words ending in -tion

acquisition, action, addition, affection, allegation, alliteration, alteration, ambition, ammunition, application, assumption, attention, auction, audition, automation, aviation, caption, caution, commotion, competition, composition, conception, condition, constellation, constitution, consumption, convention, conversation, definition, destination, destruction, direction, duration, education, emotion, evolution, expedition, fraction, friction, function, ignition, inspection, intention, invitation, junction, lotion, mention, motion, nation, notion, nutrition, observation, occupation, operation, opposition, oration, option, petition, portion, position, precaution, preparation, production, proportion, question, radiation, reaction, recreation, reduction, relation, repetition, reputation, revolution, solution, station, tuition, vacation

Words ending in -tial

confidential, essential, impartial, influential, initial, martial, partial, potential, sequential, substantial

Words ending in -tious

ambitious, cautious, conscientious, infectious, pretentious

Words ending in -tient

impatient, patient, quotient, sentient

Words ending in -tience

patience, sentience

Words ending in -cia

Marcia, Patricia

Words ending in -cian

electrician, magician, musician, optician, physician, politician

Rule	-ant	-ance
Vowel says /ə/	1 entrant 2 compliant 3 predominant	1 allowance 2 significance 3 preponderance
i says /ee/	-iant	-iance
	1 variant 2 brilliant 3 luxuriant	1 defiance 2 alliance 3 insouciance

Figure 26.3 -ant vs. -ance words

Words ending in -cion

coercion, suspicion

Words ending in -cial

artificial, beneficial, commercial, crucial, facial, official, provincial, racial, social, special, superficial

Words ending in -cious

audacious, conscious, delicious, ferocious, gracious, precious, suspicious, unconscious, vicious, vivacious

Words ending in -cient

ancient, deficient, efficient, sufficient

Words ending in -cience

conscience

What about all the -ance words?

There are also several additional rows and columns that can be examined but are not complete. The first instance is all the words that end with -ance. Figure 26.3 shows how they can be generated. When reaching the <ti> says /sh/ and <ci> says /sh/ rules, there are no more examples, or very few – certainly not enough to justify a place on the generator proper ('negotiant', 'officiant').

The word 'insouciant' does not count as a <ci> + -ant ending, as the <ci> does not usually say /shənt/ here; it says /see-ənt/.

That said, there are certainly a lot of -ant/-ance suffixes. How does one choose over -ent/-ence?

There are several observations that you can loosely base a spelling choice on:

- If the base ends with the sound /g/ as in 'elegant' or the sound /k/ as in 'significant', -ant is applied. Contrast that with the second sound of the letters <c> and <g>, /s/ and /j/, as in the words 'innocent' and 'intelligent'.
- If the base ends with <y>, the return of Illegal <i> (Chapter 25) prefers to be accompanied by -ant or -ance: 'defy/defiance', 'comply/compliance', 'rely/reliance'.
- Bases ending in expanded Wacky Rs (Chapter 20), such as <ear> and <ure>, prefer -ant/-ance endings: 'clear/clearance', 'endure/endurance'.
- Bases ending in -ve prefer to be followed by -ant/-ance ('connivance', 'grievance', 'deviant') and in fact rarely take -ent ('insolvent' 'fervent') and never take -ence.

Sorting through the wordlist below will certainly yield some useful generalisations. It is also an opportunity to test your thinking as to which technique to use in teaching these words.

Personally, I know which ending to use through practice and observation. I know that I will be right most of the time if I'm unsure and I choose -ent/-ence. There are slightly more -ent/-ence endings than -ant/-ance because -ent/-ence can also go with <ti> and <ci>.

The list below is for your convenience ('conveniance' just doesn't look right).

performance, balance, importance, finance, distance, insurance, advance, appearance, circumstance, significance, assistance, resistance, alliance, entrance, substance, allowance, acceptance, instance, enhance, assurance, maintenance, attendance, ambulance, relevance, guidance, compliance, inheritance, ignorance, renaissance, romance, nuisance, utterance, clearance, surveillance, tolerance, resemblance, allegiance, acquaintance, disappearance, abundance, variance, dominance, reassurance, reluctance, imbalance, annoyance, avoidance, elegance, grievance, appliance, reliance, brilliance, ordnance, deviance, resonance, countenance, fragrance, conveyance, reconnaissance, intolerance, remembrance, observance, arrogance, impedance, inductance, extravagance, reflectance, hindrance, provenance, severance, governance, vengeance, defiance, semblance, deliverance, endurance, remittance, ordinance, penance, admittance, temperance, vigilance, irrelevance, pittance, predominance, reappearance, issuance, radiance, valance, preponderance, concordance, conformance, conductance, continuance, dissonance, insignificance, encumbrance, covariance, pursuance, repentance, perseverance, parlance, nonchalance, abeyance, exuberance, forbearance, sustenance, furtherance

Then there's <si>

Worth mentioning here is another limited set of endings that can be generated using <si>. Figure 26.4 illustrates.

What is interesting in this table, is that <si> has two distinct sounds, depending on the base. It can make a quiet /sh/ sound, like the sound we make to tell others to be quiet. It can

Rule	-a	-an	-on
	-sia	-sian	-sion
si says /sh/	Russia	Prussian hessian	mission fission recession
si says noisy /sh/ or /ʒ/	Asia	Indonesian Persian cartesian	vision propulsion exclusion

Figure 26.4 <si> endings

also make a noisy /ʒ/ sound like the sound we make when impersonating a vacuum cleaner or other noisy, humming machine. It is made in the same manner and place as /sh/ but picks up voicing from the preceding sound and continues to be voiced. Contrast how the <si> sounds in 'vision' and 'mission'.

The <si> ending only goes with three key endings. There are few words ending with -sial ('controversial' and some scientific words). There are even fewer ending in -sious; 'transient' and 'transience' are the only examples of -sient/-sience endings.

Interestingly, the set of -sion words comprises a relatively large list, as follows:

Quiet /sh/

aggression, apprehension, aversion, dimension, diversion, excursion, extension, fission, impression, mansion, mission, omission, oppression, passion, pension, percussion, permission, possession, procession, profession, propulsion, provision, recession, revulsion, session, suspension, transmission, version

Noisy /sh/ or /ʒ/

aversion, collision, conclusion, confusion, corrosion, decision, diversion, division, erosion, exclusion, excursion, explosion, fusion, illusion, inclusion, invasion, occasion, persuasion, revulsion, television, version, vision

Both, depending on personal preference

aversion, diversion, excursion, revulsion, version

Key row	-a	-an	-on	-al	-ous
gi says /j/	-gia	-gian	-gion	-gial	-gious
	nostalgia paraplegia	Glaswegian Belgian	contagion legion religion region	collegial vestigial	contagious prodigious prestigious sacrilegious

Figure 26.5 <gi> endings

And finally ... <gi>

Another limited set of endings can be generated from the key row and <gi>. Figure 26.5 illustrates.

The letters <gi> can go with most of the key suffixes from the main Suffix Generator, though not with the last two: -ent or -ence.

Suffix Generator spelling drill

Level 1

1 arena
2 urban
3 reckon
4 dental
5 famous
6 garment
7 silence
8 mania
9 Indian
10 scorpion
11 serial
12 furious
13 gradient
14 action
15 initial

Level 2

1 oppression
2 reputation
3 ambitious
4 religion
5 detergent
6 generous
7 pentagon
8 retina
9 eloquence
10 historian

Level 3

1 incidental
2 simultaneous
3 communion
4 terrestrial
5 hypochondria
6 iridescent
7 unconscious
8 occupation
9 pretentious
10 paraplegia

27 More fascinating patterns

Throughout this book, I have tried to give an idea of what needs to be known in order to understand the basis for all spelling. There are other patterns that I haven't produced lessons for, but I hope that I have shown that, in the presence of the basic knowledge contained within previous ones, further lessons are self-generating.

This chapter lists some of my favourite patterns. They can be turned into lessons at any time by using the techniques and tools introduced prior to this.

These lists are only a small part of the ever-growing network of families and patterns that will hopefully continue to exist in your classrooms and in the minds of your students.

The Floss Rule

There is a rule that states that the letters <f>, <l>, and <s> tend to double up in a certain environment. It's known as The Floss Rule, as the word 'floss' contains all the relevant letters and demonstrates the rule. It goes like this:

RULE: Double the <f, l, s>

- at the end of a word
- but only after a single vowel
  Examples: 'off' vs. 'golf', 'fill' vs. 'foal', 'moss' vs. 'moos'

Using the Consonant Start Card, students can generate word families based on this form.

<i> before <e> except after <c>

This is the 'supreme, and for many people solitary, spelling rule' in the wonderful words of Edward Carney (1994). Indeed, '<i> before <e>, except after <c>' has helped many. Useful too is the creation of a word family based on the feature '<i> before <e> exceptions'.

Pedants take great delight in listing all the exceptions to the rule. The fact that there are arguably more words that break it than conform to it must give spelling reformists some encouragement. We ought to bear in mind, though, that there are good reasons for broken rules, and in terms of usefulness, the '<i> before <e> …' rule has much to offer in terms of a rule of thumb.

Let's look at the exceptions using the word stories worksheet (Chapter 3) and a word family (Chapter 4).

Feature: <e> before <i>, not after <c>

Family 1: Most words that have an /ay/ sound

abseil, freight, beige, surveillance, eight, feign, feint, geisha, heir, inveigh, neighbour, obeisant, sheik (not American English), skein, sleigh, rein, veil, vein

Family 2: Most words that have an /ie/ sound

eider, Einstein, either, feisty, kaleidoscope, poltergeist, Rottweiler, seismic, sleight, zeitgeist

Family 3: Words that don't have an /ay/ sound or an /ie/ sound but just go ahead and break the rule anyway

foreign, forfeit, heifer, leisure, protein, seize, surfeit, their, weir, weird

The /ay/, /ie/ addition helps to reduce exceptions to the core rule. The remaining common words can fit into the exceptions worksheet.

Absolutely not included, to the inevitable disappointment of many, are words from the following categories. To triumphantly suggest that they break the rule whilst ignoring the very clear, simple reason for this is just silly:

1 Words where an affix and a base element cause the <e> and <i> to be adjacent ('reintroduce', 'being').
2 Words where <e> and <i> are adjacent but in separate syllables ('atheist', 'spontaneity').
3 Very uncommon words ('milreis', 'seif').
4 Uncommon scientific words, which litter the world of chemistry, biology, and physics but are rarely seen or heard in normal human discourse ('seborrheic', 'Cepheid').

<dge>

It's fairly well understood that we use <ge> to make a /j/ sound where we can't use <j> (Chapter 13: Illegal Letters). This is the case at the end of words like 'badge', 'bridge', etc. and also at syllable boundaries, e.g. 'bludgeon', 'fidget', etc.

That makes sense, I hear you say, but what about the <d>? That's just there to annoy people, right?

You tell me. Let's remove the <d> and see what we get:

badge/bage

bridge/brige
knowledge/knowlege
judge/juge
bludgeon/blugeon
fidget/figet

What is the function of the letter <d>? Without it, all the vowels before the letter <g> say their names (Chapter 14: The single vowels). They *have* to be stopped.

Those vowels have to be separated from Final Silent E or from the edge of an open syllable cliff.

Furthermore, the letter that separates them from a fate worse than death has got to sneak into that position - seen and not heard, like a Victorian child.

The only letter that can do this is <d>. Feel the similarity of tongue-placement when you say /d/ as in 'dam' and /j/ as in 'jam'. Not much of a commute from /d/ to /j/, is there?

<tch>

Similarly, <tch> words would also suffer from vowel naming if it weren't for the similarly placed <t> before <ch>. Single syllable words like 'itch', 'batch', 'fetch', 'blotch', and 'catch' seem fine on their own until a vowel suffix comes along. Compare:

batches/baches
fetching/feching
itchy/ichy
blotchy/blochy
crutches/cruches

Now you've got to admit, that's beautiful, isn't it?

28 Some delightful lists

Though I am a big fan of having students compile their own word lists, it never hurts to have some ready-made ones. These can be used either for teacher reference or to form a basis for more pattern analysis.

I could include several hundred lists with thousands of words, and since we have such wonderful online resources at our fingertips nowadays, it would be a simple operation. But it's also too easy to get overloaded with irrelevant information. See Facebook for example.

I have therefore included a number of lists that I think are very relevant and very useful. I hope they give yet more insight to this, our elegant orthography.

Single letters in order of commonality

etaoin shrdlu cmfwyp vbgkjq xz

The silent letter families

‹b›

aplomb, bomb, climb, comb, crumb, debt, doubt, dumb, jamb, lamb, limb, numb, plumb, subtle, succumb, thumb, tomb, womb

‹c›

abscess, ascend, crescent, descend, disciple, fascinate, fluorescent, incandescent, isosceles, luminescent, miscellaneous, muscle, obscene, resuscitate, scenario, scene, scent, scissors

‹d›

handkerchief, sandwich, Wednesday

‹g›

align, assign, benign, campaign, champagne, cologne, consign, design, feign, foreign, gnarl, gnash, gnat, gnaw, gnome, gnu, reign, resign, sign

‹k›

knack, knapsack, knave, knead, knee, kneel, knell, knew, knickers, knife, knight, knit, knob, knock, knoll, knot, know, knowledge, knuckle

‹m›

mnemonic

‹n›

autumn, column, condemn, damn, hymn, solemn

‹p›

psychology, pneumonia, pseudo, psychiatrist, psychiatry, psychotherapy, psychotic, receipt

‹u›

baguette, biscuit, build, buy, circuit, disguise, guard, guess, guest, guide, guild, guile, guillotine, guilt, guy, guitar, guy, meringue, rogue, vogue

‹w›

awry, playwright, sword, wrack, wrangle, wrap, wrapper, wrath, wreak, wreath, wreck, wreckage, wren, wrench, wrest, wrestle, wretch, wretched, wriggle, wring, wrinkle, wrist, writ, write, writhe, wrong, wrote, wrought, wrung, wry

‹gh› words

The letters 'gh' go together fairly commonly in English words. Mostly they are leftovers from our Germanic heritage. Apart from silent ‹h› words, 'gh' combines with the preceding vowel or vowel digraph to form a new grapheme.

These graphemes fit into five main categories:

Silent ‹h›

Afghan, aghast, burgh, dinghy, ghastly, ghee, gherkin, ghetto, ghost, ghoul, gingham, yoghurt

‹igh›

bight, blight, bright, fight, flight, high, height (viewing the ‹e› as silent), knight, light, might, nigh, night, plight, right, sigh, sight, slight, sprightly, thigh, tight, wright

<ough>

/aw/ – bought, brought, fought, nought, sought, thought, wrought
/ow/ – bough, drought, plough, slough, sough
/uff/ – brougham, chough, enough, rough, tough
/oe/ – dough, furlough, though
/off/ – cough, trough
and then there's 'borough', 'lough', 'through'. Word family, anyone?

<eigh>

eight, freight, neigh, neighbour, sleigh, weigh

<augh>

aught, caught, distraught, naught, onslaught, draught (just for fun).

Last, but not least, we have 'straight'. This is very common, left over from the Middle English past participle of 'stretch'.

29 A suggested spelling and handwriting scope and sequence

Though *Spelling for Life* is aimed at a middle primary audience, the scope and sequence here covers foundation year onwards. This year has various names the world over (*prep, foundation, kindergarten, reception* etc.), but it means the first year of formal schooling, when children are around five years old. The purpose of including this and the next two year levels in this scope and sequence is to outline the foundational knowledge and skill every child needs in order to become a proficient speller.

It is necessary, also, to integrate spelling lessons with handwriting lessons. None of these aspects of written language are separate from one another. It is also recommended that all writing activities, wherever possible, centre around delivering a knowledge-rich curriculum. For instance, if students are studying the weather, they should be encouraged to spell words, compose sentences, and attempt paragraphs on that subject during spelling lessons. Integration of skills and content has been shown to be a richer, more sustainable approach to education than separating and compartmentalising (Wexler 2019).

How the scope and sequence works

Each year level is split into a number of units of focus activities. It is recommended that, in the foundation years, a high-quality systematic synthetic phonics program is implemented simultaneously.

At the end of each year level, there is a section to remind teachers to check for understanding of key principles before moving on. This is repeated at the beginning of the next year so that new intake and possible lapses in long-term memory are addressed before starting the next year's knowledge-building.

There will be the inevitable occasion when children need to catch up on the core knowledge presented in the *Spelling for Life* continuum in order to progress at their year level. This may be due to prolonged absence, being new at the school, or being in need of more intensive support.

A possible solution for schools is to have a Tier 2 unit dedicated to catching up, containing small groups of children with similar knowledge gaps.

FOUNDATION

UNIT 1
Introduce correct posture and pencil grip with the chant: '1 2 3 4 Are your feet on the floor? 5 6 7 8 Is your back nice and straight? 9 10 11 12 This is how our pencil's held.'
UNIT 2
Introduce the concept of drawing circles by orienting children to the clock face, starting at 2, going up and around through 12 and 6 and back up to 2. Introduce the concept of 'the direction in which we read and write'.
UNIT 3
Practise large and small circles on mini whiteboards and paper. Orient children to base line, middle, and line above on lined paper.
UNIT 4
Introduce the concept of straight lines, and practise drawing them on the board and on paper.
UNIT 5
Now you can start applying knowledge of circles and lines to the graphemes in your phonics program.
UNIT 6
Introduce the concept of dots at the end of sentences and above letters <j> and <i>.
UNIT 7
Introduce the concept of crossbars going in the direction in which we read and write.
UNIT 8
Introduce the concept of capital letters for special words. Orient students to the capitals in their names, at the beginning of sentences in their readers, and in storybooks. Begin developing meta-language for formation of capitals.
UNIT 9
Introduce the <q> rule and practise with target words from units of study.
UNIT 10
Introduce the <c> rule and practise with target words from units of study.
UNIT 11
Introduce the <g> rule and practise with target words from units of study.
UNIT 12
Introduce the concept of counting syllables and practise with target words from units of study.
UNIT 13
Introduce the difference between vowels and consonants and use students' names to illustrate 'a world without vowels'.

UNIT 14
Revise structure of 'high frequency irregular words' from your phonics program and begin compiling word families to teach and practise these.

UNIT 15
Introduce the concept of Illegal Letters, and start to learn the chant, 'i, j, q, u, v, at the end of a word they cannot be!'

UNIT 16
Introduce the concept of Final Silent E. Caution: 'split digraph' is not linguistically accurate. If your phonics program incorporates this language, it may be worth revising this.

UNIT 17
Introduce Final Silent E Job 2: changing the sound of <c> and <g>.

UNIT 18
Introduce the single vowels saying their names in open syllables.

UNIT 19
Introduce the concept of prefixes, using open syllable prefix re- and closed syllable prefix un- to change the meaning of bases.

UNIT 20
Check for understanding: • Correct grip • Correct posture • Correct formation of all upper- and lower-case letters • The difference between vowels and consonants • Capital letters, full stops • The <q> rule • The <c> rule • The <g> rule • Illegal Letters • Final Silent E Jobs 1 and 2 • Open and closed syllables • The concept of prefixes

YEAR LEVEL ONE

UNIT 1
Check for understanding: • Correct grip • Correct posture • Correct formation of all upper- and lower-case letters • The difference between vowels and consonants • Capital letters, full stops • The <q> rule • The <c> rule • The <g> rule • Illegal Letters • Final Silent E Jobs 1 and 2 • Open and closed syllables • The concept of prefixes

UNIT 2
Practise spelling plurals with -es, i.e. after -x, -sh, -ss, or -ch, ('foxes', 'wishes', 'glasses', 'beaches').

UNIT 3
Reactivate prior knowledge of Final Silent E Jobs 1 and 2 and introduce concept of adding suffixes -ing, -ful, -ed, and -ly to words.

UNIT 4
Discuss the concept of vowel suffixes as opposed to consonant suffixes and how you don't change the base of Final Silent E words when adding consonant suffixes, with direct reference to suffixes above.

UNIT 5
Introduce the concept of ad- being a chameleon (or assimilating) prefix. Use ac-, af-, and ag- to demonstrate.

UNIT 6
Make sure students know how to spell 'because'. Use its structure 'be+cause,' but also use one of the popular acronyms (e.g. 'Betty Eats Cake And Uncle Sammy's Eggs').

UNIT 7
Introduce the concept of sub- being a chameleon (or assimilating) prefix. Use suf-, suc-, and sup- to demonstrate.

UNIT 8
Introduce the concept of con- being a chameleon (or assimilating) prefix. Use con-, com- to demonstrate.

UNIT 9
Reactivate prior knowledge of Final Silent E, Jobs 1 and 2 and introduce concept of Final Silent E Job 3.

UNIT 10
Reactivate prior knowledge of Illegal Letters <i>, <j>, <q>, <u>, <v> and show how Final Silent E solves Illegal Letter problems.

UNIT 11
Revise prefix in- and show how it assimilates to bases with im- form.

UNIT 12
Introduce concept and spelling of irregular plurals 'men', 'mice/lice', 'children', 'feet', 'geese', 'teeth'.

UNIT 13
Check for understanding: • Plurals with -es suffix • Adding vowel suffixes to Final Silent E words • Chameleon prefixes • Regular and irregular plurals • Final Silent E Job 3

Additional words to start practising: days of the week.

YEAR LEVEL TWO

UNIT 1
Check for understanding: • Plurals with -es suffix • Adding vowel suffixes to Final Silent E words • Chameleon prefixes • Regular and irregular plurals • Final Silent E Job 3
UNIT 2
Reactivate prior knowledge of single vowels and introduce additional sounds.
UNIT 3
Begin Word Stories wheel and add to this over the course of the year.
UNIT 4
Start applying The Spelling Formula to polysyllabic words.
UNIT 5
Reactivate prior knowledge of Final Silent E and introduce Final Silent E Job 4 (giving the last syllable a vowel in consonant + -le words).
UNIT 6
Begin to look at alternative spellings for consonant + ‹l› + ‹e› endings (e.g. final, label, evil, etc.).
UNIT 7
Begin Consonant Start Cards and take time to observe the kind of consonant usually in the second position in word-initial clusters.
UNIT 8
Begin Consonant End Cards and take time to observe the kind of consonant usually in the second position in word-final clusters.
UNIT 9
Introduce the letter ‹y› and its roles in words.
UNIT 10
Check for understanding: • All sounds represented by single vowels • Word stories for irregular words • The Spelling Formula • Final Silent E Job 4 • Consonant cluster constraints • The letter ‹y›

Additional words to start practising: months of the year and colours (these are common but tricky in many cases).

YEAR LEVEL THREE

UNIT 1
Check for understanding: • All sounds represented by single vowels • Word stories for irregular words • The Spelling Formula • Final Silent E Job 4 • Consonant cluster constraints • The letter \<y\>
UNIT 2
Introduce concept of vowels + \<r\> and how this letter changes the sound of a preceding vowel.
UNIT 3
Introduce sound change of vowel + \<r\> + Final Silent E.
UNIT 4
Introduce language for cursive and begin practising basic joins.
UNIT 5
Introduce The Vowel Generator.
UNIT 6
Introduce advanced joining in cursive. Begin to guide all students to use cursive handwriting in all single-word dictation tasks.
UNIT 7
Introduce the concept of strong and weak syllables and practise identifying them in target words from units of study.
UNIT 8
Introduce concept of schwa and how it is often represented in weak syllables.
UNIT 9
Introduce 'Last 3 CVC' lessons.
UNIT 10
Check for understanding: • Wacky Rs • Cursive formation • The Vowel Generator • Strong and weak syllables • Schwa • Last 3 CVC rules

Additional words to start practising: cardinal numbers.

YEAR LEVEL FOUR

UNIT 1
Check for understanding: • Wacky Rs • Cursive formation • The Vowel Generator • Strong and weak syllables • Schwa • Last 3 CVC rules
UNIT 2
Introduce the Return of Illegal <i>.
UNIT 3
Introduce The Suffix Generator and begin compiling the chart.
UNIT 4
Introduce additional Suffix Generator patterns.

Additional words to start practising: Ordinal numbers, mathematical vocabulary.

By this time, given a good grounding in the concepts that came before, and interleaved with a robust morphology and grammar curriculum, only a handful of children will continue to struggle with spelling.

In addition to valid, reliable spelling and phonological awareness assessments, you can also check for understanding in struggling/new students with this quick rules list. Using error analysis from formal and informal word-level spelling assessment, you can see which spelling rules and conventions your students cannot yet apply.

30 Spelling for Life Quick Rules List

QUICK RULES LIST
Every syllable in every word should have at least one vowel letter.
‹Q› is always written with the letter ‹u›.
When ‹c› comes before ‹e›, ‹i›, or ‹y›, it MUST say /s/.
When ‹g› comes before ‹e›, ‹i›, or ‹y›, it MAY say /j/.
You may not use ‹i›, ‹j›, ‹q›, ‹u›, or ‹v› at the end of words. They are illegal.
When a vowel is at the end of a syllable, it may say its name.
When you cannot use ‹e›, or ‹i›, use ‹y›.
Final Silent E can make a vowel say its name, even if it has to jump over a consonant to do it.
Final Silent E can make ‹c› say /s/ and ‹g› say /j/.
Final Silent E stops word from ending with Illegal Letters.
Final Silent E can give the last syllable a vowel.
A consonant plus -le cannot be split at the end of a word.
Final Silent E can stop words looking like plurals.
When you add a vowel suffix to a Final Silent E word, drop the Final Silent E.
When a vowel comes before ‹r› it goes wacky.
‹e›, ‹a›, ‹r› inside a word often makes a Wicked Sister sound.
When ‹w› and ‹or› go together in a word, the ‹or› often makes a Wicked Sister sound.
When ‹w› and ‹ar› go together in a word, the ‹ar› often makes an /or/ sound.
In words of more than one syllable, there is always a strong syllable.
The vowel in the weak syllable is often /ə/, schwa.
Schwa can replace any single vowel in a word.
When reading and spelling long words, look out for prefixes and suffixes.
When you add a vowel suffix to a Last 3 CVC word, you must double the final consonant in the base.
When the final syllable is strong and acts like a Last 3 CVC word, double the final consonant in the base when adding a vowel suffix.
When adding a suffix to a word-final ‹y› word, return ‹y› to ‹i›.
When returning ‹y› to ‹i› and adding the suffixes -th or -s, you must add ‹e›.

APPENDIX 1
Forgive me, Scotland

Please note that the example words in this book relate to a standard accent spoken by people who populate the British Isles in the majority, i.e., the South-Eastern English.

Fine though that may be, I must declare that I am Scottish and I do not talk like that. Here is my vowel system:

Manner	Explanation	Sounds	Example words
ROUNDED	The lips are not wide open and not pulled back, but pushed forward to varying degrees.	/o/ /aw/ /oa/ /oo/	got law goat boot *and* put
UNROUNDED	The lips are not wide open and not pushed forward but pulled back, to varying degrees.	/e/ /i/ /ee/ /ay/	get sit tree day
OPEN	The lips are wide open and not pulled back and not pushed forward.	/a/ /u/	bat gum
DIPHTHONGS	The vowel sound begins rounded, unrounded, or open but ends elsewhere.	/ue/ /ie/ /oy/ /ow/	due die boy cow

/ar/, /er/, /ir/, /or/, /ur/ are all two sounds, a vowel and a consonant. South-Eastern English, Australian, New Zealand, and South African people pronounce <er>, <ir>, and <ur> as the same single vowel sound. Not that there's anything wrong with that. Scots just generally don't.

Please feel free to fit the vowels of your particular regional variation into these categories, which will remain four in number, as you will see.

If I have failed to take into account your particular accent in any part of this book, it is not for reasons of discrimination, so please don't be upset. I am a Scot, living in Australia, who many times has had the pleasure of teaching American literacy programs to people from New Zealand. Believe me, I know how it feels.

APPENDIX 2
The Triangle Game

In the early stages of spelling development, learners mainly rely on what they hear. They begin to develop and test assumptions based on letter-sound correspondences and start to apply their phonic knowledge to their writing.

Some learners progress more slowly than others due to the fact that they can't tell the difference between a letter sound and a letter name.

Errors like 'dp' for 'deep', 'mpty' for 'empty', and 'confs' for 'confess' are typical indicators of this confusion.

To screen for this and, ultimately, to eradicate it, we play the Triangle Game.

Skill level

For anyone who can say the alphabet. You can teach the letter-sound correspondences as you play.

Materials

Magnetic letters, a picture of a triangle (Figure A.1)

Duration

Five minutes at the start of a lesson. It does not take long for learners to gain a full, conceptual understanding of the difference between a letter sound and a letter name.

Example lesson

> To help you work out the difference between a letter sound and a letter name, we're going to play a game. Knowing these differences will help you become a stronger speller and reader.
>
> We talk and think about writing in three different ways. We're going to show those ways by using three different points on a triangle.
>
> The first point is the 'symbol' part. A symbol is something that we see which stands for something else. For instance, if you think about the sound /a/, what symbol do you see?

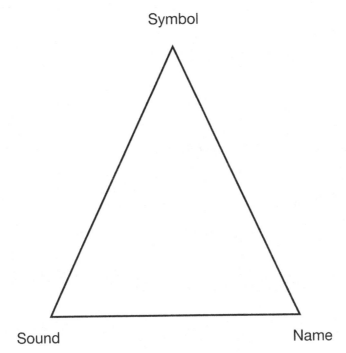

Figure A.1 The Triangle Game

Let your student write the letter <a> or pick it out from a group of letters. Place or write the symbol on the top point of the triangle.

When you see that symbol, there are two other things that you can think of. First is the sound that symbol makes when it's in words. What sound? (/A/)

Move the <a> symbol to the bottom-left corner of the triangle.

This is the sound corner. It represents the most common sound we make when we see a symbol.

We can also think of the name of that symbol. For instance, what is the name of this letter? When you're saying the alphabet, what does this one make you say? (<A>)

So let's move the symbol across to this corner. What do you think this corner is called? (THE NAME CORNER)

All three corners of this triangle are different. Let's try another one. How about this symbol?

> Pick out the letter <p> and put it at the top point of the triangle and start moving it bottom-left.

What sound? (/P/)

What name? (<P>)

How about if we started on one of the other corners this time? Let's start in the sound corner. Pick out the symbol for the sound /m/. Now move it to the name corner, what name? (<M>)

Now let's start in the name corner. How about the letter <e>? Pick out the symbol and tell me the sound.

You can go around the triangle rapidly, starting at any point. You can do this for any symbol, even those with two letters. For example, the sound /th/ requires two symbols and the naming of the two letters <t> and <h>.

APPENDIX 3
'Why not just make spelling simpler?'

For centuries, there have been vocal advocates of spelling reform, including Benjamin Franklin, George Bernard Shaw, Charles Darwin, and notably in recent times, the Duke of Edinburgh.

Spelling reformists call for a simplification of various words (e.g. 'bought' to 'bot') and for an alphabetic system that provides a greater sound-to-symbol match. Whilst I sympathise with the sentiment driving the view, I cannot support the movement.

Pinker (1994) states that through a set of rules, English words are predictable 84% of the time.

It is not hard to deal with the rules. It is also relatively easy to devise a system whereby most of the other 16% can be accounted for and learned using simple strategies familiar to most teachers.

How spelling evolved

For clarification, a brief history of our orthographic system might be in order.

English, in its written form, has gone through a process called *standardisation*, that is, 'the process ... by which standard forms of a language are established' (Matthews 1997).

With standardisation, groups can achieve their communicative purpose by eliminating ambiguity and focusing on the message (the meaning) rather than the messenger (the words carrying the meaning).

Standardisation was a means of 'setting in stone' the accepted spellings of the words of the language.

Standardisation has taken place over many centuries, during which time English has undergone several major and minor changes due to certain forces.

The major word stories

Minor changes still occur over long periods of time, due to new words entering the language via one of seven major paths as explained in Chapter 3.

The words in the 'old' category exist because of their age and commonness. These bend the core rules because their spelling has stayed true to their original pronunciation, but their sound has changed more rapidly ('was', 'there', most words where final <e> is silent and not functioning, etc.).

The beginning of standardisation

Let us begin, then, in Anglo-Saxon times, when the use of the Roman alphabet increased rapidly. Using this alphabet to encode English words already had difficulties, in that the Roman alphabet did not match, on a 1:1 basis, the sounds of the Anglo-Saxon oral vocabulary (e.g. there is no one symbol for the sounds /sh/ or /th/). Already the alphabet was being adapted to accommodate these discrepancies.

1066 and all that

The prevalence of this version of English in written documents was massively reduced following the Norman Conquest, when French scribes prevailed and brought with them their own alphabetic norms (e.g. 'fruit', 'journey', 'guard', etc.).

In the 1200s, as London superseded the seat of Wessex in matters of government, the language changed again to reflect the shift in pronunciation.

The late 1400s then saw a greater movement towards standardisation. Advances in printing and paper manufacturing at this time meant that storing and retrieving the written word became easier. Coupled with the growth of schools, standardisation blossomed.

During that time, printers became more independent of church and state, and grew in number and influence. As a means of reducing labour and costs, they were heavy proponents of standardisation.

The Great Vowel Shift

It could have ended there, and if so, we might have a more phonically regular sound-to-symbol match today. In the 1500s, however, spoken English underwent a process termed 'The Great Vowel Shift'.

This was a major change in English pronunciation, especially of vowels. Because of the process of standardisation, however, the spellings of many words remained the same whilst the pronunciation changed.

Various reasons for this change itself are put forward by linguists, anthropologists, sociologists, and suchlike, but the cause remains speculative.

The result was, however, some disparity between standardised spelling norms and pronunciation. This counts for a good section of the alleged 'random' spellings we see today.

One clear example is the existence of the letter <e> at the end of words (Final Silent <E>). In many cases, <e> is a pronunciation signal or at the very least a solution to a potential violation of a core rule. In some cases, <e> has no discernible function at all and is indeed a leftover from the Vowel Shift.

You can read all about Final Silent <E> and its functions in Chapters 16 to 19.

The final significant events

The publication of the *King James Bible* in the early 1600s and the American Revolution in the late eighteenth century were to act as great forces in standardisation and in the development of spelling as it is today.

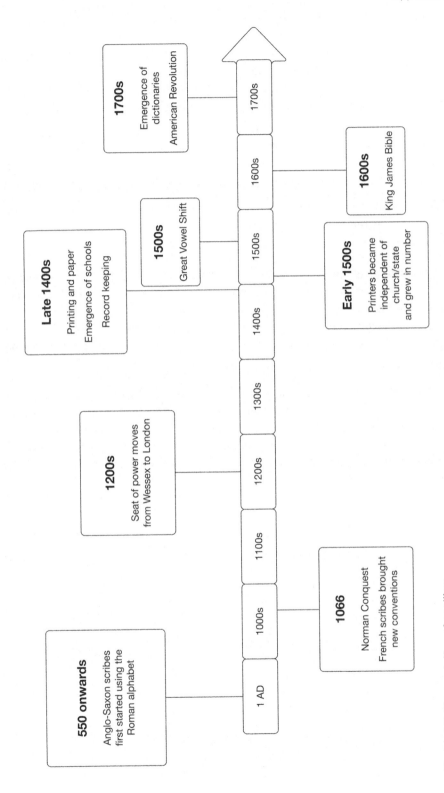

Figure A.2 The evolution of spelling

The publication of dictionaries throughout this time also helped to standardise spelling. Noah Webster, the compiler of *Webster's Dictionary*, in particular, was a very successful spelling reformist, many of whose recommendations gave the final touches to modern spelling. Webster's changes at that time include 'waggon' to 'wagon', 'musick' to 'music', and 'gaol' to 'jail'.

Being the compiler of a dictionary is a powerful way to have your version of a 'simpler' orthography realised. Spelling reform advocates before and since have had less luck.

> Time alone insensibly wears down old habits and produces small changes at long intervals, and to this process we must all accommodate ourselves, and be content to follow those who will not follow us.
>
> (Thomas Jefferson in response to a spelling reform proponent in 1813)

Their lack of success is not only to do with their lack of power, but also with the abundant obstacles any spelling reform proposal inevitably faces.

Some key points against the reform of English spelling are:

- Any new system would invalidate and/or make difficult to read any pre-existing documents.
- It is often an advantage to know where a word comes from in order to grasp its meaning. This could be lost through the process of simplification.
- The cost of bringing about such radical, rapid change would be enormous.
- Regional variations in accent prevent us from ever having one grapheme for one phoneme.

Moreover, the human brain is an enormously capable organ, more than adequately equipped to learn the intricacies of any writing system. Spelling success, then, is more a matter of teaching, through logical, sequential steps, the regular and less regular patterns of spelling. Though I sympathise with those who struggle with it, I can't quite bring myself to call for reform, and I will never accept the defeatist notion that spelling is unlearnable for some. Improvement is always possible.

GLOSSARY

base The simplest possible meaningful word-unit with no prefixes or suffixes; e.g., the removal of the prefix and suffix from the word 'unclearly' leaves the base 'clear'. This cannot be reduced any further.

common ending The last syllable of a word which appears in many other words but does not necessarily convey a common meaning. For instance, the words 'terrible' and 'table' have the same final syllable, but not for the same reasons. 'Terrible' is from the Latin root 'terrere' (frighten) and the suffix -ible (a variant of -able, used on certain types of base words). 'Table' is not a base word and a suffix in the same way, but is a derived form of Latin 'tabula' (plank, tablet, list).

consonant A sound produced with some obstruction along the vocal tract.

digraph A single phoneme spelled with two letters, such as <sh> or <oo>.

grapheme A character in writing that cannot be reduced any further. Every letter of the alphabet is a grapheme, but these can be combined to form units, e.g. <sh>.

Illegal Letters The letters <i>, <j>, <q>, <u>, and <v>. They are called illegal because they are not permitted to appear in the word-final position in English words.

lexicon The unique store of words possessed by an individual.

medial (as opposed to *word-internal*) Exactly in the middle.

mentalese 'The language of thought in which our conceptual knowledge is couched' (Pinker 1997). This can be contrasted with our lexicon, which is a store of words, but not the rich network of information that mentalese represents.

morpheme The smallest meaningful word-unit. 'Eating' has two morphemes, the base 'eat' and the suffix -ing.

morphology The study of meaningful word units, such as prefixes, bases, roots, and suffixes.

mnemonic A memory device, such as a sentence or story to aid recall of certain facts/spellings etc., e.g., Rhythm Helps Your Two Hips Move.

neural network An interconnected group of brain cells, rather like a community of people.

orthographic mapping The process by which written words are stored in memory for automatic retrieval.

orthography The spelling system of a language.

phoneme The smallest possible unit of sound. The word 'pat' has three phonemes, in that it can be broken into three separate units. The word 'path' also has three phonemes, the units /p-a-th/.

phonemic awareness   The ability to perceive the number, order, sameness, and difference of sounds within words.

phonology   The study of the sound system of a language and the relationships within.

prefix   A letter or letters added before a base to form a new, related word.

root   The earliest known origin of a word.

schwa   A mid-central, unrounded vowel often present in unstressed syllables. Phonetic symbol: /ə/.

standardisation   The formation of agreed standards of a language.

suffix   A letter or letters added after a base to form a new, related word.

syllabic consonant   Though there is disagreement among linguists that syllabic consonants exist, they can be defined as consonant sounds which form the voice impulse in a syllable, e.g. the <m> in 'spasm'.

syllable   A unit of sound produced with one impulse of the voice.

syntax   The study of grammatical relations between words and other units within the sentence.

target word   The word, in a particular lesson, that is being examined.

trachea   The hollow tube starting in the lungs and going into the mouth through which air passes.

universal   A linguistic feature that is present in all human languages, e.g. verbs, vowels, etc.

vowel   A sound made with no obstruction in the vocal tract.

word-final   At the very end of a word.

word-initial   At the beginning of a word.

word-internal   Neither at the beginning nor at the end of a word, but inside it.

BIBLIOGRAPHY

Carney, E. (1994) *A Survey of English Spelling*, London: Routledge.

Chomsky, C. (1970) 'Reading, Spelling and Phonology', *Harvard Educational Review 40*: 287-309.

Chomsky, N. and Halle, M. (1968) *The Sound Pattern of English*, New York: Harper & Row.

Dale, E. and Chall, J. (1948) 'A Formula for Predicting Readability', *Educational Research Bulletin 27*: 11-20: 37-54.

Denham, K. and Lobeck, A. (eds) (2010) *Linguistics at School*, Cambridge: Cambridge University Press.

Ehri, L. C. (2014). Orthographic mapping in the acquisition of sight word reading, spelling memory, and vocabulary learning. *Scientific Studies of Reading*, 18(1), 5-21. https://doi.org/10.1080/10888438.2013.819356

Ellis, A.W. (1993) *Reading, Writing and Dyslexia: A Cognitive Analysis*, 2nd edn, Hove: Lawrence Erlbaum.

Engelmann, S., Haddox, P., and Bruner, E. (1983) *How to Teach Your Child to Read in 100 Easy Lessons*, New York: Simon & Schuster.

Higbee, K.L. (1996) *Your Memory: How It Works and How to Improve It*, 2nd edn, Cambridge, MA: Da Capo Press.

Hudson, R. (1981) '83 Things Linguists Can Agree About', *Journal of Linguistics 17*: 179.

Kilpatrick, D. A. (2016). *Equipped for Reading Success*. Casey & Kirsch Publishers.

Labov, W. (1994) *Principles of Linguistic Change, Internal Factors*, Maiden, MA: Blackwell.

Lindamood, P.C. and Lindamood, P.D. (1998) *The Lindamood Phoneme Sequencing Program for Reading, Spelling and Speech*, Austin, TX: Pro-Ed.

Marinus, E., Jong, P., & Leij, A. (2012). Increasing word-reading speed in poor readers: No additional benefits of explicit letter-cluster training. *Scientific Studies of Reading*, 16, 166-185. https://doi.org/10.1080/10888438.2011.554471

Matthews, P.H. (1997) *The Oxford Concise Dictionary of Linguistics*, Oxford: Oxford University Press.

Moats, L.C. (1995) *Spelling: Development, Disabilities and Instruction*, Baltimore, MD: York Press.

Nagy, W., Anderson, R., Schommer, M., Scott, J., and Stallman, A. (1989) 'Morphological Word Families in the Internal Lexicon', *Reading Research Quarterly 24*: 262-282.

Nagy, W. and Anderson, R. C. (1984) 'How Many Words Are There in Printed School English?' *Reading Research Quarterly 19*: 304-330.

Nichols, R. (1985) *Helping Your Child to Spell*, Reading, UK: University of Reading.

Oxford English Dictionary (1989) Vol. 3, Oxford: Clarendon Press.

Pinker, S. (1994) *The Language Instinct*, New York: Penguin.

Pinker, S. (1997) *How the Mind Works*, New York: Penguin.

Share, D. L. (1995). Phonological recoding and self-teaching: Sine qua non of reading acquisition. *Cognition*, 55, 151-218.

Smith, N. (1989) *The Twitter Machine*, Oxford: Blackwell.

Spalding, R. (1990) *The Writing Road to Reading*, 4th edn, New York: William Morrow.

Trask, R.L. (1996) *A Dictionary of Phonetics and Phonology*, London: Routledge.

Wells, J.C. (2008) *The Longman Pronunciation Dictionary*, London: Pearson.

Westwood, P. (1997) *Commonsense Methods for Children with Special Needs*, 3rd edn, London: Routledge.

Wexler, N. (2019). *The Knowledge Gap*. Penguin Group USAWolf, M. (ed.) (2001) *Dyslexia, Fluency and the Brain*, Austin, TX: Pro-Ed.

Yates, F.A. (1966) *The Art of Memory*, Chicago, IL: University of Chicago Press.

INDEX

Page numbers in *italics* indicate figures.

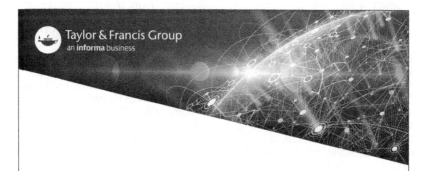

Made in the USA
Columbia, SC
09 July 2024